27810223

DATE DUE

MAY 0

To Touch Your Heart

To Touch Your Heart

Ronald K. Grooters, M.D.

*Students of Buena Vista,
Learn to go with the
flow of life and always
do good for each other.*

*Best Wishes!
Dr Ron Grooters*

VANTAGE PRESS
New York

FIRST EDITION

Copyright © 1993 by Ronald K. Grooters, M.D.

Published by Vantage Press, Inc.
516 West 34th Street, New York, New York 10001

Manufactured in the United States of America
ISBN: 0-533-10242-1

Library of Congress Catalog Card No.: 92-80321

0 9 8 7 6 5 4 3 2 1

To those who touched my life

Contents

Foreword

It's not likely that many books about hearts and surgery were conceived the way this one was, in a steamy, hot room filled with laughter, warmth, leotards, schoolbooks, and toe shoes. Tired from work, Ron Grooters and I would arrive each evening at the Des Moines Ballet school, slump into a tattered old couch, exchange a few pleasantries, and then slip into silence for a while, alone with our thoughts or absorbed by our daughters' dancing in the adjacent studio. Eventually, we'd start chatting, and inevitably the talk would wind its way to one of Ron's dreams. It was idle talk at first.

"You know, Gene, I'm thinking about writing a book about heart surgery, about my experiences as a heart surgeon, and how those experiences could benefit people."

"Great, Ron. Good idea," I'd reply, not paying much attention.

I wasn't very interested. I had plenty of work and plenty of projects of my own. Gradually, however, I realized how passionate Ron's feelings were, how firmly he believed that a book about his experiences could entertain, educate, and inspire while helping many people.

Ron explained that he and 4,000 other heart surgeons perform more than 300,000 heart bypass surgeries every year. Another 1 million patients have some other kind of heart treatment. Almost everyone has at least one close friend or family member who has either died of a heart attack or had heart surgery. Millions of Americans, perhaps a majority, are concerned about heart disease. They're taking up running or joining health clubs, cutting back on red meat, and buying low-fat frozen dinners called Healthy Choice.

My interest grew with each passionate speech, and soon my answer to Ron's insistent question—"Would you be interested in writing the book with me?"—went from, "Maybe I can find somebody who would be interested," to, "Yes, definitely. Let's get started."

And so we did, working in our spare time on evenings, breaks, and weekends, getting together to write and talk. Ron would dictate thoughts into a tape recorder—between surgeries or while making a long drive to join his father and brother for a northern Minnesota fishing trip. He'd give me the transcriptions. We would talk, I'd take notes, and then I'd sit down and write.

I spent time with Ron, touring Iowa Methodist Medical Center in Des Moines, making rounds with him, and watching him perform routine (is there such a thing?) heart surgery. It wasn't routine to me. Here is what I wrote following my experience in the operating room:

"To the untrained eye, the operating room seems like a chamber of horrors: a large room bathed in cold, white light. A flabby body of a pale white man, spread naked on his back on a long, narrow table. Cold, still, looking more like a corpse than a living human being. Women dressed in smocks, masks, and hats joke and laugh like harpies, attaching tubes and wires. One grabs the man's limp penis, stretches it high in the air, and inserts an opaque gray plastic tube (a catheter), shoving it deeper and deeper through the mouth of the organ. So routine, so hideously casual. Another slathers a sickly colored orange-yellowish-brown foamy liquid over the man's pale white skin, then wraps him in something like cellophane. They laugh, they giggle, they talk about dates, supper, and children's colds. Then Ron walks in, dressed in smock, mask, and hat, with microscope-like lenses mounted on space-age headgear.

"He takes a small blade and begins to cut the skin between the man's breasts—a long vertical cut from the base of the breastbone to the small curve at the center of the collarbone. He discards the knife and chooses a yellow plastic instrument with a wire at one end and a point at the other. He takes this cauterizing knife, which looks like some kind of electronic pen, and deepens his cut, creating fine smokey wisps and the scent of singed flesh. The nurses watch intently as Ron cuts more deeply, exposing a thick layer of globular white fat. This man has lived well.

"Ron works quickly, cauterizing as he goes to limit the bleeding. Upon reaching the bone, he trades the yellow plastic knife for a small, fine circular saw. He cuts down through the center of the breastbone—difficult at first, using muscle to get it started. Whine. Like a sheet of plywood he slices the bone. Once apart, the left side of the rib cage is pried up, clamps are attached, and the breastbone is pulled up and away from the man's chest cavity.

"Ron works quickly, locating and isolating the mammary artery behind the left side of the breastbone. The first clamps are removed and a larger retractor is moved into place and used to part the breastbone, cranking it open to expose the shiny gray membrane encasing the heart. Cutting the membrane, Ron unveils the heart, still faithfully pumping blood through this pale white male's arteries.

"The heart has to be stopped while Ron operates. He accomplishes this by inserting tubes attached to a heart-lung machine into the man's circulatory system, while the man's heart is still full of blood and pumping. Gradually, the machine takes the pumping load, and the heart is cooled and drained—put on ice, so to speak—with an injection; then ice water is poured right on the heart. The heart deflates and ceases to beat as it empties and cools. It turns pale and seems to die. Blood pumps through the heart-lung machine, through the tubes, and through the man's body, bypassing the man's resting heart and providing the vital oxygen needed to keep his brain and other organs alive.

"With the heart's functions suspended, Ron begins his work. In this case, there is an obstructed artery on the left side of the heart. Usually, such arteries are on the surface and easy to find. This one isn't. It is down inside the muscle, beneath the fat. Very hard to find.

"Suddenly, the chatter and joking stops. The room grows serious, the silence broken only by intent discussion and commands. This 'routine' operation is no longer so routine. Fine probes are used to search for the hidden artery. Precious time passes. The room grows more tense. A fifteen-minute task stretches past thirty. Finally, after much sweat and silence, the blocked coronary artery is located and the healthy internal mammary artery is spliced in with fine microscopic stitches, providing a bypass around the obstruction in the coronary artery and a new route for a safe supply of blood to the heart. Forty-five tense, lifesaving minutes and the task is complete.

"Slowly, the man's heart is warmed and brought back on line. Another tense time. The longer a heart is kept in suspension, the greater the danger it won't recover; forty-five minutes is an awfully long time. Slowly, slowly, however, the man's faithful heart returns to normal. The heart stabilizes. Tension eases. The machine is disconnected. The breastbone is wired back together, the skin stitched. The operation is over. The man will slowly return to consciousness in his hospital bed, just a bit sore, remembering nothing of these outwardly bizarre, lifesaving minutes."

During months of sessions at the hospital and weekend retreats in our homes, I came to know Ron— the man and the surgeon. And over those months, his thoughts and ideas and his fascinating, entertaining story took form on my home computer screen— progressing from a young, mischievous boy to a reflective, philosophical surgeon.

Ron was born and raised in Boyden, a small farm town in northern Iowa. During his formative years after World War II, his father and maternal grandfather ran a blacksmith shop that eventually blossomed into a farm-machinery business owned and operated by Ron's dad. Big tractors and combines, heavy machinery, the smell of grease and welding fumes. Ron loved that world. One of his fondest memories is of his grandfather teaching him how to make a good, strong weld joint.

His favorite world, however, was a finer, more delicate world. It didn't take long for Ron to show a love and aptitude for science, medicine, and surgery, areas he explored with curious, sometimes mischievous, exuberance.

At an early age, he conned his father into a surgical

fiasco involving the postmortem examination of a pet hamster. Ron got high. His blacksmith father got sick when the cut into the still-warm hamster's abdomen produced a squirt of foul-smelling blood and tissue juice. There were other adventures, too, involving microscopes, women's underwear, explosives, snakes, and neighborhood pets.

Still, there was no one around prescient enough to see his destiny. Ron himself thought he wanted to be a glamorous air force fighter pilot, a "top gun" if you will, although that term wasn't used back then. He might have gone that route, too, if it hadn't been for substandard eyesight and a miserable performance on a U.S. Air Force aptitude test.

Instead, Ron went off to Iowa State University, where he thought he'd earn an engineering degree, and then perhaps have another shot at military flying. Nope. The aptitude and interest in math just weren't there. After a couple of months of spending every waking hour pushing a slide rule and solving equations, Ron "began to see engineering as a career devoid of human interaction, a career filled with hours at a drafting table or desk with a pencil, calculator, and graph paper," Ron recalled. No people! Nothing warm and fleshy to relate to. Just working with numbers, equations, and calculators. "That might be right for some," Ron thought, "but not for me."

Science, especially biology, was a different matter. This was about the mysteries of life and living things— things like the hamsters, snakes, and frogs Ron loved and carried around in his pockets as a child. A couple of premedicine friends opened this world to Ron. He looked ahead and saw himself "working with and helping people while making a good living."

Ron's years in medical school at the University of Iowa were filled with triumphs, fiascos, trials, and tribulations. There were long nights of study, wild parties, and sometimes humiliating sessions with members of the medical faculty who didn't always appreciate Ron's exuberant but sometimes cavalier approach to the study of medicine. He survived, however. Indeed, he thrived, despite some lapses in concentration and judgment. Ron's first surgery was a simple procedure—stripping varicose veins from an overweight woman's legs. It was a bloody, messy, ripping, and tearing operation. In his excitement, he almost cut himself with the scalpel. Nevertheless, he had discovered the "thrill of surgery," the simple, straightforward, ego-building, healing power of the knife.

Ron discovered as he matured, however, that there is more to surgery than the clean cut of a knife. He came to realize that the flesh and blood belong to people—people with hopes, dreams, problems, and fears. As he grew and matured in general surgical training and eventually as a heart surgery specialist, he began to focus more on the whole person. Over the years, performing thousands of heart surgeries, he also came to realize that his surgical practice thrives because Americans live abusive lives. They smoke too much, drink too much, eat too much, and drive their blood pressure up with high-pressure lives filled with tension. Opening people up day after day, year after year, and seeing arteries clogged with fat or torn from high blood pressure took its toll, eventually building to the point where Ron wanted to start shouting at these people, "Stop! Stop ruining your bodies! Stop tearing your bodies and lives apart!"

Over the years, he also discovered that not all surgical programs are created equal. While most, probably 90-plus percent, are excellent, some do have better results—less bleeding and fewer infections and other complications. Some are better than others, and the better ones are not always the ones with the biggest names or the highest profiles.

So here is Ron's story, from his childhood adventures to his shouting message about your heart and how you should care for it. It's a compelling story— partly because he is so typical of thousands of surgeons who fix hundreds of thousands of broken hearts every year—but also because Ron is an extraordinarily caring surgeon who is constantly searching for new ways to care for his patients—and for his patients to care for themselves. He has invented a device that has cut the risk of stroke during heart surgery to almost nothing. He has discovered ways to drastically cut infection and other complications related to heart surgery. And he is working on a new design for an artificial heart.

His book will help heart patients and their family members understand heart surgeons and heart surgery. Perhaps more important, it will teach people to take control of their lives in a way that will make them happier and healthier.

Everyone should find this book entertaining, informative, and beneficial.

—Gene Erb

Acknowledgments

This book would not have been possible without the thousands of cardiac surgeons and cardiologists who have dedicated their lives to promoting and improving heart care. Their unending work, their pleasant and unpleasant clinical experiences, combined with countless hours of research, have made it possible for me and my contemporaries to provide top-notch heart care. I especially thank and commend Dr. Carl Almond, my chief in residency, and Dr. Salim Saab, his assistant professor, for putting up with and training me at the cardiac surgery program in Columbia, Mo. I realize now the difficult task these pioneers in our field had.

I cannot forget other close colleagues who have touched me. Dr. Louis D. Rodgers, a general surgeon, was so instrumental in my surgical training and encouraged me to continue my training in heart surgery. Dr. Chad Williams and Dr. David Lemon, outstanding cardiologists, were first to help my first partner, Dr. Hooshang Soltanzadeh, and me start the open heart program at Iowa Methodist Medical Center. Now many other excellent cardiologists, Drs. Javad Yans, Dirk Ver Steeg, Craig Stark, and Jim Lovell, have joined them over the years, and another outstanding group of cardiologists from the Iowa Heart Center, Drs. Mark McGaughey, Phil Bear, Galen Van Wyhe and Ron Weiss, have provided essential support.

The medical team at Iowa Methodist—nurses, perfusionists, laboratory and X-ray technicians, respiratory therapists, and on and on, including my favorite building maintenance worker, Charlie—have in their own ways inspired and helped me. They often worked harder and longer than I did to provide the miracles of healing—and always with tremendous support for all of us from the hospital's administrative staff and board of trustees.

I profusely thank my partners, Dr. Soltanzadeh, Dr. Kent Thieman, and Dr. Robert Schneider. Without their unending support, camaraderie and plain common sense, this book would not have been possible.

I especially thank our secretaries, Janet Emerick, Dixie Van Syoc, Joanne Gates, and Julie Penland. They have been cheerleaders for this book, especially Julie Penland, who endured hours of my dictation and struggled to put many of my stories into words.

I cannot thank Professor Neil Harl enough for his chapter in the book—a first-person look at heart surgery from the patient's point of view.

Indeed, I thank all of my heart patients and sincerely dedicate this book to them, too. You have given me your faith, hope, and trust while overcoming fears and anxieties, waiting for a surgeon to hold your heart in his hand, hoping to have it fixed.

Mr. Gene Erb will be forever remembered. This book would not have been completed without his enduring expertise. He took many of my ideas, stories, and edited and molded them to make this book meaningful and inspiring. If you like this book, he deserves much of your praise. And without him, it would not have been as much fun becoming an author.

I saved my most important praise and thanks for last—for my family. Without their love and caring, my accomplishments would mean nothing. My parents, Mr. and Mrs. L.V. Grooters (Tuffy and Mina), provided the discipline, guidance and encouragement I needed to seek and meet my goals. Without their love, I would not have learned to love. So now I affirm my love and thanks to my dear wife, Kay, and my cherished daughters, Dawn, Julie, and Lori. Your support, attention, and encouragement, while at times I paid more attention to this book than to you, could only come from unconditional, understanding love. I truly, from the bottom of my heart, dedicate this book to you. Kay, Dawn, Julie, and Lori, I hope "to touch your heart," not just with this book, but with each day God gives me.

To Touch Your Heart

Seeds of a Surgeon

I should have seen my calling when I was eight years old, standing next to a blacksmith named Tuffy in a dimly lit basement. That's right, a blacksmith and repairman named Tuffy, a man accustomed to the hard ring of the ball peen hammer and the scorching cut of a flaming torch. There we stood—me watching wide-eyed, and Tuffy, my father, poised with a dull paring knife, ready to cut into the distended belly of my pet hamster. The hamster had died, despite our efforts to keep it alive. It had been sick for some time, perhaps a week or two, its abdomen enlarging day by day. My father and I thought it was a female. We thought it was pregnant. We worked to keep it warm and healthy. We fed it with an eye dropper to keep it alive.

We lost our first patient. No mother. No live birth. To tell you the truth, I was more upset about missing the live birth than I was about the death of the "mother." As a matter of fact, I was so intrigued, I wanted to have the hamster opened to see; I wanted to see the babies inside. I wanted to see why the hamster had died. So there we stood, my father and I, poised for our first operation.

My father felt he should be in charge. I remember him running upstairs and asking mother for "instruments." She gave him a dull paring knife and an old pair of scissors that wouldn't cut paper. She didn't want him messing up anything good. She wasn't thrilled by this episode, anyway, and she sure didn't want a mess, not even in our basement.

The operating room was musty in a pungent sort of way, full of the odor of ripe potatoes trying to sprout. The operating "table" was a warped, scratched workbench with a crack down the center, tools in the back, and a vise at one end. Cobwebs stretched between the rafters, lacing an assortment of hanging tools. One dim light bulb caked with dust cast shadows on the carcass.

I was oblivious to the cobwebs and dust. The pungent, musty smells didn't exist. All I could see was that furry, stiff body filled with mysteries. Would there be babies? Would we find what killed the poor little creature, despite our efforts to keep her alive?

Dad took the first plunge. Grabbing hold of the skin with pliers that had been hanging above, he tried to poke the point of the knife through the abdomen skin. It was tougher than he had expected, and he had to strain to push the dull knife in. A final thrust, and then a squirt of rancid blood and juice. Tuffy gagged and almost vomited, a puzzling reaction to me. Here was my father, a wiry blacksmith more than twice my size, bothered by a little squirt of foul-smelling blood and fluid. He stood incapacitated for a moment, then handed me the tools and said, "Here, you do this."

I took the tools, anxious to continue the cut, imagining I might even find some live baby hamsters. Discarding the dull knife, I picked up the scissors. I slit the skin, then the tissue, and the belly opened up. By this time, Dad had regained his composure and his curiosity, although he continued holding his nose with left thumb and index finger and kept his right hand behind his back. Perhaps he was afraid he might accidentally touch the smelly little beast. Or, worse yet, the critter might still be alive and might lunge for his hand.

There was nothing to fear. The hamster was quite dead. We'd missed the cause of death by a long shot, however. She wasn't pregnant, and she hadn't died in "childbirth." My poor little hamster had been constipated, with markedly distended bowels full of stool. Why, we would never know. I was dismayed, so much so that I continued to look for babies, probing the distended intestines with my fingers. There were none to be found. I'd missed what I thought might be my first chance at a caesarean delivery, and we'd both misdiagnosed the hamster's problem. After completing our "autopsy," I asked for some thread so I could sew the animal back together. My father ran up the stairs to find the cotton string, usually kept in one of the kitchen drawers. His running to fetch the "suture" for me gave me a delightful feeling of being in charge. I had the savvy and intestinal fortitude to complete the operation. He didn't. I could do something my father couldn't do, and I was only eight years old. A real ego trip.

Not all of my experiences with animals were so constructive. A couple of years later, around the Fourth of July, a neighbor boy and I celebrated the holiday a bit too enthusiastically with one of a neighbor woman's dozens of cats. It was a hot, humid day in our sleepy little town of five hundred, and we were in a bad humor. We were hot, sure, but mainly we were bored, even though we had firecrackers going off all around us and the town sounded like a battlefield.

A cat, which was quite friendly, happened by our little spot of shade, spawning dark thoughts in our juvenile minds. Perhaps there was some way we could include the cat in the celebration of Independence Day.

3

And perhaps we might learn something at the same time, something like: Just how powerful are those Zebra firecrackers, anyway? We decided to experiment with the cat's tail. I ran to the house and found some string, while my friend cuddled the cat. I dropped down next to my friend, out of breath with excitement.

The relaxed cat lay purring, nestled in my friend's arms, its tail sticking out beneath his elbow, wagging in a beckoning motion, inviting me to proceed. Gently we stroked the cat, and very delicately wrapped the string with the firecracker around her tail, arranging the string so the firecracker was on top where we could see it go off. We put the cat on the ground and lit the firecracker's unusually short fuse. Pow! right at our feet, and the cat was gone in a flash, straight up a tree, leaving us with a shred of fur and the cat with a partially denuded, blistered tail. We were fortunate, and so was the cat. It didn't lose its tail. We weren't seriously hurt. I don't believe our neighbor and parents ever found out.

A good thing, too, because my parents, while supportive and loving, were firm disciplinarians. Both grew up in this very strict Dutch community with strong religious convictions. There would have been hell to pay, and more fur flying, if they'd found out about the cat.

Both could be stern, but my mom was in the forefront because she was at home. I remember when I was three or four years old Mom got so frustrated with me running off all the time that she bought a dog harness, put it on me, and hooked it to the clothesline with a metal clip, the idea being that I could run all I wanted, up and down the clothesline, without getting lost. It didn't work. My freedom was lost. I was controlled and didn't like it one bit. In a fit of rage and tantrum, I shrieked with screams louder than the town's noon whistle. It attracted so much attention, with so many neighbors looking to see what was happening to me, that Mom quickly reeled me in. She was so embarrassed, she never tried that again. And I got my freedom.

Dad would do the mopping up if Mom was "frustrated." Dad was forthright, honest, and despised dishonor. If he gave his word, that's all that was needed, and he expected the same from me. If he got less, I incurred his wrath. He was extremely firm. When he got mad, his lip would flatten, stretching a scar on his upper lip left from a sledding accident as a kid. His chin would dimple. His cheeks would puff out and press against his vein-marked, bulging neck. His face would turn red, and he'd melt my soul into submission. It was a metamorphosis I seldom experienced but constantly feared. I always thought that hidden behind it all was love and understanding, but during those terrifying moments, I wasn't quite sure. Then, as quickly as his anger rose, it would melt and pass, and we'd be father and son again.

My inquisitive nature continued with a microscope and chemistry set when I was ten or twelve. The chemistry set's manual experiments quickly bored me. All you could produce was a little heat or precipitation in a test tube with a combination of two chemicals. I started looking for more exciting reactions, ones that would explode, show power, do something. I looked for formulas for gunpowder and other explosives in my parents' encyclopedia set and in chemistry books at school and the local library. I knew my parents would take away my chemistry set if they knew what I was doing, so I kept my research a secret. I found formulas for gunpowder and dynamite, then proceeded to duplicate those compounds, or I tried. I conned the high school chemistry teacher into giving me nitric and sulfuric acids, which were important in making gun cotton. I ordered powdered charcoal, sulfur, and saltpeter, without telling anyone what I wanted them for.

I made bombs in the basement. Without goggles, without gloves, but with plenty of enthusiasm, I figured out ways to make several explosive compounds and incendiary devices. One, I remember, involved melted powder sulfa and zinc encased in a small box with a fuse of cotton soaked in potassium nitrate. I set it off in the basement while my folks were away. It worked, all right, not as a high explosive but as a smoke bomb that skittered around the floor like a water bug. It filled the basement with a grayish green, foul-smelling smoke. I ran upstairs coughing, gagging, and gasping for air, pleased that the experiment worked but fearing the consequences. I opened up the house and cleaned and put away everything as fast as I could. It worked. Mom noticed a lingering smell, but she didn't say much, and I volunteered less, vaguely mentioning a chemistry "experiment" involving sulfa compounds.

Encouraged, I forged ahead, endeavoring to make gunpowder with the sulfa compound, sodium nitrate, and charcoal. I fetched the key to my dad's locked gun case from a drawer in his bedroom, where I'd seen him put it after hunting trips. I figured a little powder out of the shotgun shells in the case would help produce a particularly high explosive. I figured right. The concoction in a six-inch-long pipe from my dad's blacksmith shop dramatically changed the trash barrel behind the house, filling it full of dents and holes and splitting it apart at the seam. Dad never confronted me, but he did wonder aloud who would do such a thing. I got the message. When I think back on it now, it's a wonder I'm not responsible for taking my own life rather than saving lives. It's a wonder I have the eyes and hands I need for the delicate work I do.

My interest in science and animals took a more compassionate course after the hair-raising experience with the backyard trash can. The microscope set proved to be a lot of fun. It was not as macho as a bomb. It was a lot safer, and I did find interesting things to look at under its powerful lens—everything from feathers to the veins of leaves. I examined organisms in pond water. They looked like tiny monsters from outer space or creatures from prehistoric times. It was intriguing to watch them swim in a little drop of water. I checked out leftover food, where I was amazed to find mites on cheese. Under the microscope's powerful lens, the mold on an old loaf of bread was transformed into a mystical forest filled with trees. I was to find that there were so many living things around me that I could not see without the microscope lens.

I explored the larger world, too. I found a little bull snake, about the size of a large night crawler, near a lake on a school field trip. It was so cute, so tiny, so delicate, I couldn't resist picking it up. I carried it in my front pocket all the way home on the bus. Every few minutes I would put my hand in my pocket to make sure it was still there. It seemed to suck on my fingertip. I didn't realize it was trying to bite me. It didn't hurt. It just had a pleasant, raspy feeling. I thought the snake was enjoying being cared for in my dark, warm pocket. I was being as gentle as I could. I could hardly wait to find a place for it at home, to feed it and watch it grow. I knew Mom wouldn't like the idea. Dad wouldn't care, but I knew he'd take Mom's side. So I kept it a secret as long as I could. With the snake still in my front pocket, I made a small cage out of an old wooden peach carton. I remember Mom yelling down to me in the basement, "Ron, what are you doing down there?" "Oh, nothing. Just making a little box." She didn't ask what the box was for, and I didn't think she'd ever find out. I fastened a screen on the box with wire brads. It wasn't as tight as it should have been, but I put the snake in anyway and set it on the workbench behind some paint cans. I came back the next morning and the snake was gone. It had gotten out, and so did my secret when I asked Mom what happened to the snake. I thought maybe she had thrown it out.

"What snake!" she exclaimed. "You had a snake in the house, and now it's loose in the house?" She was almost hysterical and disgusted and angry at the same time. She was upset. No doubt about that. I was upset, too. I was upset because my snake was missing. I imagine Mom was upset because she thought the snake might end up in a pile of dirty clothes on the basement floor, under her pillow, or, even worse, next to her while she was sleeping. We never found the snake.

Not all of my animals were unwelcome guests. I frequently found injured animals and brought them into the house to nurture them back to health with Mom's help. Many died, but a young mourning dove with a broken wing survived after weeks of care and feeding. I kept it in the hamster cage and secretly hoped I would be able to keep it as a pet. I realized when it recovered, however, that I would have to let it go. I did, and every summer thereafter we had a mourning dove in our backyard. I always wondered if it was the one I had saved.

All of these things—the poor distended hamster, the explosives, the tiny bull snake, the injured animals, and the items under the microscope—excited my inquisitive nature, heightened my curiosity, and satisfied my appetite for exploring the living world. Those fun times eventually led to my pursuit of science and medicine, but not without some detours. In fact, I never thought at all about becoming a physician until I was well into my first year of college. Like most boys, I dreamed of being a fireman, a farmer, or an airline pilot. I thought of joining my father's farm machinery business, something he adamantly opposed. He wanted me to get the education he never had, believing there was little future for me in his blacksmith, repair, and machinery business.

I also thought a lot about having fun—playing baseball and softball, running track, dating. These were paramount in my life during my high school years. As with most youngsters, the mysteries of girls and the changes in my own body dominated my inquisitive energies during adolescence. I noticed the new hairs sprouting on my body and assumed that they somehow signaled my passage from childhood. It was all guesswork, however. Parents didn't explain much when I was young, and we sure didn't have sex education in school. I was so ignorant, I didn't even know what Kotex sanitary napkins were. Stacking them as a stock boy in the local grocery store, I assumed they must be something you used on special occasions, something you put on your dining room table on a

9

Sunday after church. Gradually, this knowledge void was filled in the informal trial-and-error way of the day.

My interest in girls blossomed, but my success with the opposite sex lagged considerably, at least until my senior year. I was a scrawny little squirt, about a hundred pounds, when I started high school. In fact, I might have been called a nerd or a geek if kids had been using those words. I was still interested in math and science, and had an inferiority complex because of my small size that kept me in constant trouble with my peers. I was a little wiseass full of wisecracks. Fortunately for me, most of the time the guys I ridiculed couldn't think, or run, nearly as fast as I could. I struggled through high school in that fashion, striving for attention and pining over girls. In my senior year, an attractive, vivacious brunette named Edna caught my eye. We dated steadily, I was crazy about her. She seemed to be the one for me. But like many high school romances, it didn't last after I went away to college.

I took a test for entrance into the Air Force Academy during my senior year, hoping to become a glamorous military pilot. I failed miserably, not even passing the preliminary test. A friend of mine from a neighboring town, a boy I played basketball against, was the lucky one. He passed the test and was accepted. I was so jealous and disappointed. I thought he was the luckiest boy on earth, not knowing that eight years later he would be killed in combat while flying over Vietnam. He left two little girls behind. That could have been me, if I had made the grade. Reflecting back on that helps me realize that the roads we choose, the things we think are so important, are not always the best. I truly believe that some force—destiny, for want of a better word—pushed me away from the glamour of

the Air Force Academy and into premedicine at a state university.

I thought I would study aeronautical engineering at Iowa State University, join the ROTC, and then join the air force and become a dashing, macho pilot. My eyesight began to weaken, however, and I soon discovered that studying all the math and physics necessary for an engineering degree was boring and laborious. My first few months at Iowa State I felt chained to my desk with nothing but a slide rule, graph paper, and numbers for company. I began to perceive engineering as a career devoid of human interaction, a career filled with hours at a drafting table or desk with a pencil, a calculator, and graph paper. I wasn't happy, and two of my friends at Iowa State—both in premedicine—could see it. They encouraged me to consider premedicine, a curriculum filled with interesting biology and chemistry classes, general science, social studies, and some math. I didn't think consciously about it at the time, but I think my subconscious remembered all the fun I had as a boy, playing with my chemistry set, my microscope, and my animals. It didn't take much to persuade me to change majors, especially when my friends reminded me that doctors make good money. That, to be quite frank, had something to do with my decision to enroll in premedicine. I looked ahead and saw myself working with and helping people while making a good living. I went to my counselor in aeronautical engineering and told him I wanted to make a change.

"What do you want to change to?" he asked.

"Premedicine," I replied.

"Oh," he said, "you want to be able to buy airplanes instead of make them."

The Sprouting Surgeon

Premedicine was my oyster—a place to make my pearl. My grades improved from B's and C's to A's and B's. I padded my grade point with chemistry and biology. I had a deep inner feeling that I had made the right choice. I felt sure I would get into medical school, not realizing how competitive it would be, not worrying about the trials ahead. Ignorance was bliss.

I studied hard in those premed days, but I also played. Every Friday night, four of us guys would sit up and play the card game 500. Jim was the all-American boy in our group, good-looking but only average at cards. Otto was a chubby, talkative Bohemian who had no common sense at the card table. And Gordy was a little piker of a guy with a Jimmy Durante nose, Coke-bottle bottoms for eyeglasses, and the uncanny ability to win game after game, although many times cheating to do it. Around dawn, we'd go out for breakfast and then return to the dorm and sleep for a few hours before getting up for the day.

I say I studied hard, but I also found that if I attended class religiously and listened intently, I could discern what each professor considered important. As a result, I had a "gift," a knack for knowing what would be on a test. I didn't study nearly as hard as some of my buddies because I felt I knew what would be on the test. Professors and instructors would give clues. Paying attention and picking up on those clues probably helped me more than anything to get the grades I needed for medical school.

English and the humanities were difficult, but chemistry and the biosciences were easy. In chemistry and other science courses, I frequently didn't even bother to buy the text. I just studied my classroom notes, and occasionally borrowed a text or checked one out from the library.

I applied at just one medical school, the University of Iowa's, in my junior year, not thinking that they might turn me down. Another case of blissful ignorance.

I took the entrance exam and made it, much to the surprise of many in my small hometown, who remembered a scrawny, misfit high school kid. One man told my father, "He'll never make it. You have to be a doctor's son to get in."

Being accepted into medical school was glorious—praises back home, congratulations from all my friends and relatives. It was a bit amusing, too. That summer, people in my hometown started asking me medical questions and telling me about their ills, as if being merely accepted into medical school made me some kind of an expert. I knew nothing. More ignorance.

That summer, I played softball and baseball, drank beer, and generally had a good time as my mind wandered into the future. At times, there was terrible apprehension, a feeling that I had to produce, I had to make it. Still, I had no idea how difficult it would be—the late nights, one after the other, studying until one, two, or three in the morning.

That fall, I joined Phi Rho Sigma, a medical fraternity in a dilapidated old house. The fraternity was not a winner, structurally or socially. The house was dusty and dirty. The windows were rotting and falling off, and the wind howled through the uninsulated walls. The place was so bad, I was too embarrassed to take a date back to the house. Sure, it was a dump, but I figured the associations and camaraderie would help me. I was counting on the fraternity's old tests on file, and I figured the older students could guide me through. It did help. At the same time, it was torture because students in your class would quiz you and you would quiz them, trying to stump one another. These quiz sessions would go on to the point of absurdity—trying to scare each other into overstudying. Most of us caught onto the game after a few weeks and settled into serious study. A few, however, continued to study the minutiae, staying up until 4:00 A.M., popping caffeine pills, and drinking gallons of coffee. Some of those students burned out then dropped out.

I remember one in particular, a little Chinese student from Jamaica (really!). He was so nervous: wide eyes, shaky hands, apprehensive voice, nervous laugh, always bothering everyone, including me, knocking on my door, checking to see what I might know that he didn't. The poor guy invited abuse, like a buzzing gnat. (We knew what his problem was, but it still pissed us off.) He was out of control. Any time he missed one of our absurd questions, he'd run back to his room to look up the answer. We soon learned to search for ridiculous details in our medical texts and then ask him, knowing he'd be stumped. It got to be a contest to see who could rattle him the most. He flunked out in his third year. He was so nervous, he couldn't steady his hands enough to draw blood for lab tests. Instead, he faked the results, entering made-up numbers on patients' charts. Eventually he was caught and expelled.

Several students, some of them very intelligent, burned out and dropped out from worry. Fortunately, most of us had the sense to study the basics and learn them well. I tried not to worry needlessly or put myself under stress. As a result, I didn't burn out, and my grades were above average.

One fellow student took that "no stress" approach to the extreme. He went an entire semester without ever studying human physiology. He spent almost all of his spare time playing bridge. He came to me in tears the night before the final; he knew he didn't know anything and was going to flunk out. What made it worse for him is that he didn't want to be in medical school, anyway, and his father was head of dermatology. Still, he hoped against hope that I could help him through.

I told him what I thought would be on the test. As it turned out, there were essay questions on the test related to each of the areas I had outlined for him. He got all of the essay questions right, and missed only some of the multiple-choice questions. He scored an 81 on the test after studying three hours, a higher score than most of the others who had been studying all along. He's now a successful dermatologist in Indiana or Illinois and doesn't have much need for human physiology.

Medical school required a lot of booking, but it also involved a lot of "playing doctor." For example, I remember one poor elderly man at the university hospital who had to suffer through almost a dozen proctological exams of his prostate gland as each student, one after the other, probed his posterior. I was about ninth in the line of examiners. God, I hated that.

There was a certain amount of role-playing required, too. You had to feign keen interest, even if it didn't exist, or the resident physicians and staff physicians would assume you lacked motivation and load you with more work or lower your grade. I learned the hard way while rotating on the orthopedic surgery service with a chief senior resident named Macbeth. The name conjured up images of distrust and rebellion for me, and the man lived up to the name, at least in my eyes. I thought he was arrogant. He didn't explain things very well, and he seemed to have an irritable disdain for students, as if they were impeding his important work. His attitude rubbed off. I worked with a chip on my shoulder and didn't do all of my work. Wow! Was I surprised when I got called into the orthopedic staff office at the end of my rotation, read the riot act, and grilled on the spot. It quickly became apparent that I hadn't studied the material. There I was, sitting in front of a faculty orthopedic surgeon, stumbling and stuttering with every question. The professor seemed witchlike to me—in his late fifties, with a graying beard and a crow's beak framed by shot-glass lenses. He fired questions at me in a high-pitched voice, almost with a cackle. No doubt I deserved every minute of it. I was given extra work and extra research to do on vitamin D-resistant rickets, just to pass the course without having to repeat the rotation. It was a lesson well learned that I occasionally forget even today—that you often have to work hard and maintain your enthusiasm, even when you don't want to. A good lesson, but difficult for me to swallow.

One of my brightest moments occurred just as I was beginning my first rotation in internal medicine. It involved the diagnosis of a case of Hansen's disease (leprosy) while examining a woman complaining of numb spots and thickened skin on her arms and back. She was a friendly, pleasant woman—thin, gray-haired, about forty or forty-five. I enjoyed chatting with her. Her ailment stumped me, however, until she mentioned that she was a missionary and had just returned to the United States from Africa. Eureka! Like a bolt out of the blue, the words I'd read just the night before came rushing back. With typical good fortune, I'd stumbled across Hansen's disease in a medical text. I had taken a few minutes to read about it because I found the disease intriguing. Of course, I didn't mention that to anyone after making the diagnosis. Everyone thought I was a genius, diagnosing leprosy in an American woman in Iowa in the middle of winter.

During these years in medical school, I had no idea I would become a surgeon, let alone a heart surgeon. I thought family practice was just what I wanted. To this day, I think I would have been happy doing that. I took extra pediatrics, internal medicine, and other family practice courses, and gave very little thought to surgery.

In fact, my first surgical experience as a junior medical student was boring, demeaning, and just plain miserable. I was assigned to assist in surgery on what we cruelly called the typical gall bladder patient: fat, fair, female, and forty. She was all four, and I had to stand for three hours just to the surgeon's left, holding a retractor—a metal device that holds the patient's incision open—while a first-year surgical resident struggled to extract his first gall bladder. He couldn't make up his mind where to cut, or where to sew and tie. He also was hindered by a seemingly insecure faculty surgeon who kept wanting to see what he was doing and getting in his way without providing useful instruction. I was constantly peppered with medical and surgery questions. I thought most were irrelevant, but in fact many covered areas I should have studied but hadn't. It seemed like a ridiculous exercise at the time. My arms ached. My legs tired. My brain went numb with boredom once the questions ceased. My mind drifted to more pleasant thoughts—of golf and girls instead of galls—and then was jolted back to the dreary task at hand by more probing questions from the surgeon. I grew so tired, disinterested, and disgusted holding that liver out of the way for three hours for what I thought should have been a thirty-minute job that I remember saying to myself after the operation: "No way I'm ever going to be a surgeon." I right then and there decided to finish medical school, complete a good general rotating internship, and then take care of patients. I had no idea that the Vietnam war and the Berry Plan would alter my life's course and change my plans.

Despite all the work, medical school was fun most of the time. We still had time for girls and wild parties. Thinking we were hotshot medical students, we drank too much, swore too much, and generally made asses of ourselves at professional fraternity parties. Professional? Yes, that's what they called our medical fraternities, but in hindsight at times I would have to question the "professional" label.

I remember one particular party at the med school's answer to Animal House, a fraternity known for taking pride in crude, shocking behavior. I knew I was in trouble with my date when I saw the bathrooms. The men's was designated with a huge penis and testes hanging obscenely above the door. The women's, equally obscene, was marked with an oversized representation of female genitalia. The house was hot and crowded, the music was loud, and the place wreaked of sweaty flesh lurching to the beat of heavy rock music.

The floors were sticky with spilled drinks, and couples groped passionately in every corner, couch, and chair. If you dared put down your drink, someone would put a cigarette in it. I discovered that the hard way, spitting a foul butt from my mouth as I finished my gin and tonic.

Just when I was beginning to think I might be able to escape with an only half-pissed date, the music died and one of the house's "brothers," a budding doctor, informed us it was time to "gather 'round" for skit time. I would have given anything to slip out of the place with my date. But there we were, trapped in the crowd with no way out. We crowded together, probably four hundred of us in a twenty-by-thirty living room, and the raunch began, culminating with a skit featuring two fraternity members dressed as Richard Burton and Elizabeth Taylor. "Richard," lying under a sheet on a gurney, was the patient. "Liz" was his nurse. In no time, of course, "she" was probing under the sheets to see what his "problem" was. She found it, and soon they were humping and thrashing on the gurney under the sheets. The skit climaxed with pants, screams, moans, and spurts of shaving cream around the room accompanied by showers of condoms thrown from the gurney. I tried to shrink and melt away into the wall. Needless to say, I never saw my date again.

We thought we had good reasons for our asinine behavior. After all, we were going to be doctors. We had to work long, hard hours, and we needed to relieve the stress. It was a rationalization, really, but we thought we needed that kind of fun.

Another form of "fun" was the *Biopsy*, an irreverent and outrageous magazine published by each senior class at the end of the year. The magazine, a medical

19

school tradition that was supposed to make money for the senior class picnic, had always poked fun at the medical school staff and had always been a bit base and bawdy. The crude, ridiculous cartoons, essays, and poems in ours outdid them all. One cartoon depicted President Lyndon Johnson sodomizing John Q. Public, with the caption, "The Great Society." One of the poems went something like: "Roses are red/Violets are blue/ Dr. So and So/ We all say screw you." It was so crude, even the university's nonmedical students were scrambling to get copies. Actually, we might have gotten by with it if we hadn't made the mistake of selling it to the general public on the downtown streets. It quickly sold out. Someone was so "impressed," we had heard, a copy ended up on the governor's desk. Hot words from the governor's office scorched the dean of the medical school and the university president. The dean immediately banned the publication and reprimanded our class officers. At the time, we thought the sanction was something you would expect in a Communist country. "It was all in fun!" we cried, but down deep in our hearts we knew we had been asking for trouble. We got it, and not just for our class. The *Biopsy* ceased publication that year. To my knowledge, it has never returned.

I started looking for internships in my senior year, still thinking of family practice. Then I did my first surgery. It was a simple procedure, stripping varicose veins from an overweight woman's legs. Large veins bulged through her skin, causing her huge legs to swell and turn purple just above her ankles. Venous stripping is a ripping and tearing operation. Students were allowed to do it because the chief resident saw our enthusiasm and liked our attitude, and I am sure because the surgery requires very little technical skill. It's performed infrequently today, although some localized vein ligations are done. At any rate, here I was in my first operation, clumsily making a small cut over the vein just above the ankle while the senior surgical resident supervised and probably held his breath. At first, I felt as if I was cutting the tissue with the handle of the scalpel rather than the blade. I almost stuck myself with the blade in my excitement and tensions. Finally, I exposed and opened the vein above the ankle, then threaded the cable up the vein. I made an incision over the vein in the thigh, through which the cable exited. I threaded the cable up the vein, with its burr on the end down by the ankle, and tore out the vein, pulling and jerking toward the thigh, as if I was in a tug of war. There was blood everywhere, but I was delighted to see I had done it correctly because the whole vein was stripped out. No one dreamed at the time that the leg vein I had removed would be vital to one of the most common operations done today, the coronary artery bypass.

I found a thrill in this surgery, and an even greater one when I did an amputation during the last surgery rotation in my senior year. Another senior medical student and I were caring for a poor little old woman, shriveled from malnutrition, with gangrene in both legs. She had been brought in for treatment from a nursing home, where she had suffered an agonizing torture of stench and pain. The staff decided she wouldn't live unless both legs were removed. So there I was, cutting away at one leg just above the knee while the other student was cutting the other. Our ability to stop the bleeding with clamps called hemostats was lacking, and there was a fair amount of bleeding. The senior surgical resident was assisting, giving us both direction and harassment, watching in amusement as we attempted to make soft tissue flaps to cover the ends of the sawed bones. One of the surgical professors poked his head in the door while we were working and wondered aloud if we believed in, or ever would learn, how to stop the bleeding. It was a joke designed to ease the tension, and it was the kind of talk I needed to hear. That, along with the experience of feeling flesh parting beneath a sharp scalpel, was all I needed to spark my interest in surgery and build my ego. I really wasn't any good at the time, but I certainly did enjoy it. It gave me a sense of power and well-being to help patients this way. It was almost an addictive high.

I was on my way to becoming a surgeon and didn't even know it. But first I would have to complete my internship at Butterworth Hospital, a medium-size private hospital in Grand Rapids, Michigan. The year was 1967. I was twenty-five years old, and I knew I could do it. As a senior, you know you can do anything. You think you have seen a lot. You don't realize you're about to discover that you know damn little.

Suddenly, I found I was a real doctor, needing to come up with real facts to make real decisions without the constant help of a senior resident or a staff doctor. I had thought out emergency situations in advance— one, two, three, a, b, c; a step at a time; think; don't lose your cool. Most of the time it worked. Most of the time it was easy, but I was always wondering if I could handle what might come next.

I saw a lot during my internship. My most vivid memory is that of an emaciated, very sick old woman, brought in lying on her belly, moaning and groaning. I was working in the emergency room at the time, a long

22

twenty-four hours on and a short twenty-four hours off. We were never able to sleep during the twenty-four hours on. And while we collapsed and slept during those twenty-four hours off, the raspy sandpaper feeling in the eyes never seemed to go away. The old woman was brought in by her daughter, who said she was very sick with cancer. What the daughter said didn't sink in until I walked into the room. There she was, lying on her stomach, covered with sheets. I pulled the sheets back and was hit by a dead animal stench that almost made me vomit. The woman's back was covered with a skin cancer, a melanoma, the size of a football. Each deep crevice was infected and oozed with foul-smelling fluid. While living alone, the woman had ignored it for years. Now she was dying. The tumor was irregular in shape, its crevices exuding pus that was running down her skin. It almost seemed to crawl. There were brown satellite lesions under the skin around the huge tumor. It was almost as if a huge prehistoric insect had latched itself to her back and was laying eggs and multiplying while devouring her little by little. We couldn't stop the poor woman's cancer or significantly prolong her life, but we thought we could make her more comfortable. She underwent successful removal of the tumor, leaving her with a huge defect on her back. A skin graft was used to line the huge crater where the tumor had been, and the infection was controlled. She died of cancer three months later because the cancer had spread to her lungs and destroyed her breathing capacity. It was not until then that I realized that medical school had taught a mere fraction of what I would need to know to be a good doctor—not just the textbook knowledge and techniques but how to deal with failure and grief.

I'll always remember the eighteen-month-old boy

who came in with a high fever. He was delirious, in shock, and semiconscious, with purple spots all over his skin. He had been feeling ill for just six to eight hours when his parents decided something serious was wrong and brought him in. There was little we could do. We administered intravenous fluids and antibiotics immediately, but they were ineffective. He died within two hours of highly contagious meningitis bacteria that had gotten into his bloodstream and caused a collapse of his cardiovascular system. The walls of his tiny blood vessels were destroyed, causing rapid, fatal shock. I remember the trembling parents grasping one another with fear and grief, tears streaming down their cheeks. They seemed to know their child was mortally ill. They seemed to know what was coming. My legs were heavy, my mind was numb, and I had a lump in my throat and tears on my cheeks as I walked with a staff doctor down the hall to a waiting room to tell the parents their son was gone. Gone so quickly, almost as if hit by a truck.

Gunshot wounds and ghetto stabbings were easy. The old man with appendicitis was easy. But the accumulation of routine and unexpectedly shocking situations provided invaluable experience.

During this time, war was raging in Vietnam, and in its own odd way this horrible war helped push me into surgery. During my internship, like every young physician at the time, I had to enroll in what was known as the Berry Plan, a draft deferment lottery for newly trained physicians designed to provide time for training in a specialty. Selection was random, with three possibilities—direct induction into the service, a one-year deferment, or a four-year deferment. I requested the one-year option, but to my surprise, I was given a four-year deferment. I was still thinking about being a family practitioner, but with that much time, I decided to take general surgical training.

I started looking for programs and found a position at Iowa Methodist, the largest hospital in Des Moines, Iowa. The surgical program there was small and struggling. It definitely wasn't a prestigious Johns Hopkins-type training program, and I wasn't all that excited about going there. At least, I figured, it gave me a place to practice surgery for four years. As it turned out, this 700-bed hospital provided much more experience and many more cases than I would have gotten as a resident at many larger hospitals with high-profile, prestigious programs.

I didn't go to Des Moines alone. Just three weeks before leaving for my surgical training in May 1968, I was married to a young woman from Council Bluffs, Iowa. Kay was beautiful and kind, and I was deeply in love. We had dated during my senior year in medical school. I knew she was the one for me. Love letters kept our passions high while she was in school finishing her degree in speech and drama and I was in my internship. She was a very stabilizing force in my life then, supporting me all the way, even during some of my most difficult, disappointing moments. To this day, she is the rock in my life.

Off to the surgery residency we went, with no place to stay, $300 in our pockets, a few clothes, a two-door '63 Chevy Impala, and an old black-and-white television set in the back.

Four years of residency seemed like a long time in the beginning, but it went quickly. It was fun and exciting, and the instruction was good. My first rotation was in gynecology. Hysterectomies were performed

25

every day. I had been there less than a month when one of the surgeons handed me the knife. I looked at him in disbelief. My vision blurred. A chill ran down my back, and my arms seemed paralyzed. "You want me to do this?" I asked. "Yeah," he replied. "It's about time."

I picked up the knife and gingerly laid it on the woman's skin, hardly making a scratch. The staff surgeon roared, probably remembering his first days as a budding surgeon, but my courage grew, and I cut the tissue down to the muscle, then through the muscle and into the abdomen. The staff surgeon guided me through the procedure. After a while, it started feeling very natural, very comfortable, even during this first surgery. Two hours later, the woman had lost her uterus and ovaries and I had gained valuable experience and confidence. The staff surgeon's patience, compliments, and reinforcement helped me realize I had made the right choice. I knew I could get even better.

People probably don't realize that the actual surgery is the fun part for the surgeon. However, 95 percent of surgery is deciding whether surgery is needed and making decisions about postoperative care. I had to learn that time and time again, and that's one of the big reasons why surgical residencies take four or five years. Many patients only worry about the edge of the knife. Unfortunately, that's all we surgeons sometimes worry about, too. You can cut, sew, and tie very quickly, but you have to be ready for the unexpected and for complications. You have to spend time with your patients, both before and after surgery, if you're going to be a good surgeon.

During my residency, I learned through practice

and by observing other surgeons. I learned the most watching and working with them on the tough cases. Every surgeon had a different technique during surgery, a different way of going about pre- and post-operative care. Basics tend to be the same, but all surgeons provide their own style and flair.

I'll never forget the young man who, four years before I saw him, had been in an auto accident and had smashed the lower lumbar vertebrae. His was a very unusual case, a situation I have seen just once in my career. He was paralyzed from the waist down. For some reason, the crushed vertebrae became infected and an intermittent bleeding hole appeared on his right flank. Every week or two, the scab would break and blood would spurt out. Sometimes a pint at a time would spurt from the infected wound. An X ray of the abdominal aorta showed a complete obstruction. Something was plugging the artery. We thought we could go in, unplug or bypass the artery, and find the cause of the intermittent bleeding.

Trying to enter the abdomen, the staff man and I were confronted with a mess we couldn't believe. The aorta, the large vessel leading into the abdomen, was nowhere to be found, buried beneath a mound of scar and fatty tissue. The bony vertebral parts that had been smashed in the accident were lying in pieces, and the aorta seemed to disappear into the morass of tissue. We probed, looking for the aorta for an hour or so, then suddenly we hit a gusher of blood that shot into our faces. The room turned pink for a while as the nurses wiped our eyes. We stuck our fingers into the hole to get control of the bleeding and our composure. The scarring was so bad, we couldn't even get a loop around to tie off the aorta, a procedure that is usually very easy. All we could do was hold our fingers on it. We felt like little Dutch boys saving the day, and it was exciting.

My arms aching, I stood there, holding the dike, while the staff surgeon searched his brain for answers. Fortunately for the patient, the answers eventually came. We used a long curved needle and suture resembling rope to close off the wound. It certainly didn't look pretty. The staff surgeon elected not to try to bypass the artery, believing that the bypass could become infected over time. He could see that nature had provided its own bypass, through all the collateral arteries around the aorta. Observing him, I was impressed to see how the staff surgeon thought through this unique situation, making decisions that were best for the patient as he proceeded. The young man did fine. We stopped the bleeding and saved his life, with several units of blood, of course. This was not a typical case, the kind of case you file in your mind for future use. But it was a good lesson for me—to expect the unexpected. You have to be able to think on your feet and find solutions in unusual situations.

I thought I had seen and experienced a lot, but I still had a lot to learn. I treated patients competently, but I treated them as if they were there for me to learn on. I didn't feel I could get close to them. I didn't touch them or help them emotionally. I just more or less worried about learning from their problems. Gradually, I began to notice the staff surgeon's concern for his patients. He took time to relate to them, to help and comfort them, their friends and family. At the time, I didn't think it was necessary, but like most surgeons, I learned its importance as my experience and wisdom grew. For me, the metamorphosis came slowly, mostly by trial and error and by observing surgeons with their patients, for there was no formal training in patient relations.

My relationship with Kay was growing and maturing, too. We decided to start a family. Halfway through my residency, in May 1970, our oldest daughter, Dawn, was born.

I was on call the night Kay went into labor. I remember finally going to bed in the hospital call room shortly after midnight. About 1:00 A.M., the phone rang. It was Kay, who thought she was in labor. The pains were five to six minutes apart and were lasting for thirty seconds. I was not concerned, I told her to go back to bed and get some rest.

I went back to bed, but was jarred awake by another ring at 2:00 A.M. The pains were four to five minutes apart and longer in duration. I gave the same advice: "Go back to bed and get some rest."

At 3:00 A.M., the phone rang again. The pains were three to four minutes apart and were lasting up to a minute. This time, Kay would have none of my doctorly advice: "You want me to have this baby at home? You come and get me, now!"

I slipped out of my surgical garb and into my street clothes, picked her up, and got her to the hospital by 4:00 A.M. Kay was hurting, but Dawn took her time. She wasn't born until eleven o'clock that night. "See, I was right, wasn't I?" I asked. Kay failed to see the humor in my remark.

Like all of the residents at Methodist, I rotated to a new service every three to six months, with intermittent assignments at Broadlawns, the county hospital. The rotations gave residents a chance to explore a wide range of situations and experiences, and to more or less try our wings. Since the hospital was relatively small, we had to explore our abilities with much less supervision than we would have had in a larger hospital. The experience provided a combination of fun, frustration, and fear, sometimes mixed with a longing to be back at a big hospital under the wing of a faculty surgeon. The experience quickly seasoned us. Humility and disappointment were always just around the corner, and difficult experiences were never forgotten.

One of my most difficult experiences involved a beautiful young woman in her early twenties who tried to commit suicide with a .22-caliber pistol after an argument with her husband. She had been rushed to the emergency room at Broadlawns in a state of shock. Her frantic husband was just outside the emergency room door as we resuscitated her and put her on IV fluids. He was outraged that a staff physician was not right there, on the spot. He kept ranting, raving, yelling, and threatening everyone as he was pulled into a different room. At the same time, there wasn't much we could do because he insisted that we delay surgery until his personal staff physician was present. There his wife lay, pale and almost lifeless with shock, as we continued to assess the situation. Precious time was passing. We had the operating room ready and the staff man was on the way. An eternity seemed to pass, but he was there in just a few minutes. The staff surgeon looked at the young woman and then talked to her husband, who was still out of control.

"Save her!" he threatened, "or I'll shoot you! I'll shoot all of you!"

With that the staff surgeon, a private physician in town who had volunteered his time to the county, glared at the man and said, "No you won't. I won't be her doctor if that's the way you're going to be." He turned and walked out!

I was her surgeon now. Sweat began to soak my undershirt and trickle into my pants. Here I was, just a junior resident, with a wild man and a dying patient with a bleeding belly wound. I didn't know if I could handle it. As a matter of fact, I thought I might not be ready for this. I not only called another staff man to help, I had someone call security and the local sheriff. I needed all the help I could get. This young woman was my responsibility now.

We rushed her down the hall, onto the elevator, and up to the operating room. Everyone was helping. Packs of replacement blood were on hand, and the team atmosphere helped relieve the tension and restore my confidence. The woman was confused and incoherent. We brought her blood pressure up with transfusions, but then it plunged to nothing when we started administering anesthetic for the surgery. My heart sank. I thought we had lost her. The nurse and the other surgical resident grabbed the hanging bags of blood and squeezed them until their knuckles turned white, forcing blood into this pale, dying woman. Her blood pressure returned to low normal as we made our first cut. Nothing bled as the knife divided the skin, fat, and muscles of her abdomen. Suddenly, she was open, and there it was—a large, pulsating, bloody bulge deep in her belly behind the bowels. It looked as angry as her husband. By now, the other staff surgeon had arrived, and now I had the nerve to go on—into the bloody mess to gain control. The big question was, could we find the bleeding point and control it before she bled to death? Where would the holes be? We quickly discovered that the bullet had pierced her aorta, liver, and pancreas. It had cut her left renal vein in two, and everything was bleeding. We struggled with the aorta. The bullet had penetrated it, both front and back, and heavy bleeding kept obstructing our view of the wound. The bleeding stopped for a moment, a symptom of shock, and I quickly began stitching the aorta. With the aorta repaired, I thought we might win, but just when I thought I had it all sewed up, something else would start bleeding. Then her heart quit. We pumped on her chest and resuscitated her to get her heart going again. Then more bleeding—from the liver this time. The wound seemed to grow, to get deeper and bloodier. Her body got colder. She arrested again. We couldn't get her back.

A shroud seemed to form around my head as goose bumps chilled my arms. Sweat ran down my back again as I realized I had to face her irate, irrational husband. I had to tell him the bad news. I didn't know if I would have to duck, run, or just stand there and take it. Would he have a gun? I gathered my reinforcements—my fellow resident, the staff man who had been there during the surgery, a security officer, and a sheriff's deputy.

As I opened the door from the operating room, the security force followed. The husband nervously stood up. I didn't know what to say, so I was blunt: "She didn't make it." Silence. All his rage turned inward. I expected to see him pull a knife or a gun, or to clench his fists and go wailing. His eyes became slits. His pupils narrowed. His lips pursed as I tried to explain to him what had happened. Instead of lunging, he collapsed into a chair in deep grief. Silence engulfed the room. Right then and there, I knew I had a lot to learn about how to handle families, how to handle relationships, how to bear bad news. I felt I had muddled through. I was disappointed. No, it hit me harder than that. I'd lost a part of myself along with the patient. All my pride left me. I was on the edge of depression. I had lost this young woman who had just had a fight with her husband.

As I gained experience and confidence, I continued to get feedback from the staff surgeon, much of it encouraging me to consider cardiovascular surgery. By my last year, all I wanted to scrub for were chest cases and blood vessel surgery. I still had a major void in my training, however. Actual cardiac surgery was not being performed at this hospital because the hospital's only heart surgeon had semiretired and had moved to a town farther north. Without any training in the specialty, heart surgery was a void in my training and far from my mind. Still, I knew I liked working with blood vessels. Blood situations were a fun challenge. They seemed to give me the feeling of a race driver pushing to the limit. If there was a hole or a physical defect that was hard to repair, I loved to be there, to see if I could repair the damage and stop the bleeding—even if failure threatened me.

Throughout my training, I saw a number of surgeons who couldn't tolerate the sight of blood. To me, a little bloodletting was the name of the game, and vascular surgery was where you encountered it. I scrubbed on as many vascular cases as I could, gaining experience handling blood vessels. One of my real triumphs involved a very thin woman with a large abdominal aneurysm, a huge dilated area caused by a weakened wall of the aorta. The staff man assisted while I repaired the damage in a difficult operation that took an hour and a half. I thought I was the greatest surgeon in the world, not realizing at the time that a damn good surgeon had been guiding me all the way.

Special Forces

As my training in general surgery ended and my time in the army approached, I knew I could handle Vietnam. In fact, in a way, I was looking forward to it. I saw it as a chance to practice surgery in a high-pressure, challenging environment. It would test my mettle and provide an intense period of surgical experience. I wanted to practice what I'd been taught over the last four years, and I thought Vietnam would provide that opportunity. Plus, I'd be working with young men— patients who could respond to surgery and therapy quickly and recover from devastating wounds. That in itself could be satisfying and make a surgeon look good.

The year was 1972, however, and just prior to the completion of my residency, President Nixon started pulling troops out of Vietnam and putting an end to the conflict. I still had orders to go there upon completion of my training at Fort Sam Houston in Texas. I soon found out from returning surgeons, however, that there would be little, if any, surgical experience there, even if I did go. Troops were pulling out rapidly. There was very little fighting, and few bullet holes needed patching.

I was anticipating disappointment but keeping my hopes up. Action was what I wanted. Still, leaving the hospital wasn't easy. The residency had been a good four years; we had made a lot of friends. I left with tears and wet palms as I shook hands and hugged my friends.

Kay and I packed our belongings and headed for

Texas with our two-year-old daughter, Dawn. The trip to Fort Sam Houston in San Antonio was uneventful until we arrived at Austin, Texas, where we stopped for the night. The next morning, Dawn had a tantrum while I was leading her to the car. In her fit of rage, she jerked away from my grip, fell, and slammed her face on the sidewalk. She split her lip and splintered a tooth, driving it into the back of her lip. Blood was all over the place. My first "action" after my residency. It didn't bother me. I was trained for such things. But Kay almost fainted. We got out handkerchiefs and put pressure on her mouth until we arrived in San Antonio, about two hours later. Dawn hooted, hollered, and cried all the way, making the two hours seem like two weeks. Her anguish and loud crying bothered me much more than the bleeding. By the time we arrived in San Antonio, the bleeding had subsided, but the action wasn't over. As we entered the city, several cars collided in front of us, throwing people and things all over the place. I slammed on the brakes, just missing the back bumper in front of me. I pushed open my door and dashed from our car to see if I could help. There was no helping anyone. The two people seriously injured in the accident were both dead, killed instantly, with blood oozing from their mouths and fractured skulls. It wasn't the kind of action I'd been looking for, either in the States or in Vietnam.

We left, feeling sad and disheartened, and drove the rest of the way to Brooks Army Medical Hospital. Dawn's mouth still needed attention. After three hours of frantic, impatient waiting, a dentist finally was available to help Dawn. He thought we should have the jammed and splintered tooth pulled. There I was again, more trauma, sitting in a dentist's chair, holding my tired, angry, screaming, kicking, biting daughter in my lap while the dentist strained to pull her tooth. Sitting there, struggling to hold Dawn still, I not only felt sorry for her, but then truly realized what families must go through when a loved one is suffering. I wondered if that is the kind of experience more surgeons needed.

Finally, the dentist managed to extract the tooth, leaving a front-and-center gap we had to look at for the next four years. Her bleeding, crying, and screaming and my anxiety subsided. We were relieved and finally ready to look for a place to stay. Our spirits sagged again, however, when we discovered that every motel in San Antonio was full. With no rooms available and the hour getting late, we drove back out of town and found a motel. Sleep was hard to come by that night. Between Dawn wanting to be held and my worrying about where we would stay the next day, my sleep center was not in command. I wished the long night would end and daylight would arrive quickly so we could see what tomorrow would bring. Tomorrow we would look for temporary housing. Tomorrow, I hoped, would be better. It had to be better.

It was, but only because the previous day had been so bad. The fan belt broke, disabling our car and causing a three-hour delay while we waited for repairs. Finally, after asking for help at a real estate office, we found a place to stay during my five weeks of basic military indoctrination. The place was a mile and a half from Fort Sam Houston, a shabby, unpainted old motel that had been converted to rental units. Its only redeeming quality, besides being close to the fort, was a clean, well-kept swimming pool. Relieved, tired, frustrated, and already wondering if army life was for us, we moved in with the stale smells, giant cockroaches, and earwigs (large wormy creatures with pincers on one end and feelers on the other). Having crustaceans as close neighbors did little for Kay's sagging morale, especially since they felt free to drop in anytime. Literally drop in. My biggest laugh for the five weeks came after hearing a shriek from the bathroom. I threw open the door with fear and trepidation, only to find Kay, covered with suds and water, slipping and sliding in an effort to scramble out of the tub and away from an earwig that had fallen from the ceiling and landed between her legs. So much for her relaxing, tension-free soak in the tub.

I roared until tears rolled down my cheeks, not knowing that the next night would bring my turn for a similar confrontation with another individual of the same species. In my case, I woke up with my friend—Mr. Earwig—on my leg. I remember feeling its testing little pinch. I reflexively threw back the covers and leaped for the light. There he was, little Mr. Friendly, about an inch long, with pincers and feelers working at both ends. Kay howled and roared with laughter until she couldn't breathe. I quickly swatted it to the floor and squashed it with a shoe. The remainder of that night, I had a hard time getting to sleep, partly because of fear of another encounter and partly because I was still stinging from Kay's uproarious, vengeful laugh. We still laugh about those nights.

At any rate, we settled in and I started my training at the fort. We learned how to shoot a rifle, how to polish brass, look spiffy, and march in formation. I made the mistake of mentioning that I'd been in ROTC in college and ended up in charge of a platoon during parade drills, frequently marching them into a wall, into another formation, or into some other predicament

38

before I could remember the word *halt!* I was ridiculed by my fellow physician soldiers, but when I offered to relinquish command of the platoon, I had no takers.

Kay was still periodically in tears, knowing I had orders for Vietnam. I would be at Fort Sam Houston a brief few weeks, and then? We didn't know. The first week of training passed quickly, but the second week was a long bore, sitting in class, trying to learn the army way. Then, sometime during that week, while walking through the mess hall area, I noticed three men at a table wearing green berets bearing medical insignia on their close cropped heads and several rows of medals on their chests. They looked like real soldiers, I thought. I had to stop to see why physicians were wearing green berets. This was exciting. I didn't know John Wayne types would be here recruiting doctors.

Yes, they were from the Special Forces. They were friendly, not mean and tough. It was simple. They needed doctors. After a brief conversation, it seemed they were interested in me, even though I had gone through surgical training and my rank, a major, was fairly high. They said they could use a surgeon to run their surgical and medical course at the Special Forces training center in Fort Bragg, North Carolina. I would be put through Special Forces training, including jump school, they said. It seemed exciting, like a great opportunity, a chance to do something different, even if it was under a parachute instead of in the cockpit of a fighter jet. Still, I wasn't sure I was in good enough shape for it, and I wasn't sure Kay would go for it.

I went back to the motel armed with the idea that I had a chance to stay in the States. I hoped that would sell Kay on the idea. I wouldn't have to go to Vietnam in just a few weeks. We could stay together for my entire army obligation. There was just one hitch. I would have to learn how to jump out of airplanes. Would Kay, always the cautious soul, buy that? I didn't know. I hoped. What I did know was that I sure would like to try jumping out of an airplane.

I meekly mentioned to Kay at supper that night that there was a unit that needed doctors. Like a boy wanting to do something his parents might not allow, I didn't tell her right away that it was a Green Beret unit, or that I would have to jump from airplanes. Eventually, I had to tell her: Yes, to join the unit, I would have to go through jump school and some other training at Fort Bragg, but I'd be able to stay in the States with her. I couldn't believe how quickly Kay agreed! It must have meant a lot to her, having my trip to Vietnam canceled, even if it did mean jumping out of a perfectly good airplane! I explained that I would be teaching Special Forces medics how to perform amputations, tracheotomies, and other simple surgeries in the animal laboratory. It was a neat opportunity. I laid it on pretty thick because I really didn't want to go to Vietnam. I didn't like the idea of leaving Kay any more than she did. Besides, I loved the idea of parachuting. Now that was right down my alley! So after Fort Sam Houston, I was off to jump school for three weeks at Fort Benning, Georgia, and on my way to becoming a Green Beret. I was starting to feel more like John Wayne all the time.

Heading for the Special Forces, I knew I had to get in shape. Kay helped in this. She knew I wasn't a good swimmer, so she pushed me into swimming. She knew I had a hell of a time doing sit-ups, so she made me do sit-ups before bed every night, almost to the point where I got mad at her.

40

It seemed to me she'd make a pretty good sergeant. I'd finish a lap and she'd say, "Come on! Keep going!"

"Kay, you're my wife!" I'd complain. But I'd continue, steaming, fuming, and glaring at her after each lap. Fortunately, I was pretty good at pull-ups, push-ups, and running. Otherwise, I might never have gotten to bed, or out of bed in the morning!

For two weeks, I worked and worked until I was so sore I could hardly sit or lie down. I didn't know how tough it would be at airborne school. Once there, I discovered I was in better shape than most, even better than most of the cadets from West Point. It kind of pissed me off, but at the same time I was glad I had worked myself into halfway decent shape. I enjoyed watching some of these young guys struggling to run a couple of miles every morning, and then do calisthenics for thirty to forty-five minutes. The old men— me at thirty-three and a major who was a pilot in the marines at thirty-four—were in better shape than most of the eighteen- to twenty-three-year-old immature "soldiers." We smugly called them "the boys."

I flew to Fort Benning after driving Kay and Dawn back to Kay's parents' home in Council Bluffs. It was a spartan army post with wooden buildings and asphalt roads stretching for miles across several jump zones. The first two weeks, we didn't see a parachute. We did learn how to fall on the ground—again, and then again, ad infinitum. The real fun exercise was a thirty-foot tower. We were strapped to a harness, then hooked to a cable similar to the static line we would be hooked to in the aircraft. We had to learn to jump from the tower in proper form with our feet and knees together, elbows in, and in a tight tuck position, the way we would from an airplane, so we wouldn't spin as we

41

came out of the aircraft and cause a malfunction of the chute. We learned to keep our chins down tight against our chests so our heads wouldn't snap back when the chutes opened. I often thought while I was standing in line to jump out of the tower, *God, what am I doing here with all these young guys? What have I done?*

My first dozen jumps off the tower were awful, with low scores and lots of ridicule from the training sergeant. After each jump, I had to report to the sergeant for a critique of my aircraft-exiting technique. When the jump was lousy, he made me drop down and do push-ups—ten at first, and when he found out I was a surgeon, he made me do thirty. That exercise continued until I could exit the tower with my feet and knees together, my elbows in, and my eyes open. It took a dozen jumps before I kept my eyes open. It just didn't seem natural to exit a thirty-foot tower, harnessed and hooked to a cable. The ground seemed to rush toward me with harrowing speed, causing my eyes to reflexively close. Of course, it was bad technique to close your eyes. Jump school instructors derisively called them "night jumps." And yes, I must admit that my first dozen or so jumps from the tower were "night jumps" in broad daylight.

What an exhausting time! Working so hard in those sawdust pits, falling down, over and over again, for hour after long hour. And then, later in the day, jumping out of the towers. I developed a boil on my buttock, right where one of the harness straps cuts, and suffered through it for the next two weeks. Every time, getting strapped in or swinging out of the tower, I cringed when the strap squeezed the boil. Damn! The hurt penetrated. Fort Benning wouldn't have been so bad if it hadn't been for that damn thing. Pus and pain were building, and I was feeling toxic and bad because of it. I needed a surgeon! Finally, gathering my nerve and not wanting to go to sick call, I took a pocket knife and jammed it into the boil while taking a shower. The pain was excruciating, but when I withdrew the knife it was instant relief as the damn thing drained and bled.

At any rate, I made it. I wasn't the best jumper in the world, but I enjoyed it. I didn't puke going out of the airplane, like a lot of the younger jumpers, and I was proud of myself. Three weeks later, I was back in Council Bluffs to pick up Kay and Dawn. Then it was back to the army and Fort Bragg, where I encountered that frustrating "hurry up and wait" syndrome familiar to so many who have been in the service. I wanted to hurry. I didn't want to wait. I had been away from surgery for three months now, and it was getting on my nerves.

At first, I was put in a dispensary with two other physicians, seeing soldiers in sick call but letting the Special Forces medics do most of the work. There was no blood in the dispensary. After six months of routine dispensary duty, the center surgeon retired. Being a major, I happened to be the next highest ranking doctor, so I became the interim center surgeon while the Special Forces awaited the arrival of a new lieutenant colonel who would take the assignment. For three months, I sat in command staff meetings, sometimes for hours at a time. It was interesting, learning what was happening in South America and the Middle East and how that might affect the Special Forces. At the same time, I felt I was sitting there with my thumb stuck up my rectum, not being able to contribute much because I had no army experience.

I was really looking forward to the assignment at the medical school and the animal lab so I could see some blood once again. Finally, the physician in the lab moved on, and it was my turn. I didn't realize, however, that I was about to enter the command of a real bulldog infantry officer with a strict, unrelenting attitude toward army regulations. He was a big man, an infantry officer and army all the way, with a fat neck and bulky body to go with his pushy personality. To make matters worse, I didn't get a chance to practice real medicine, just practice on goats in the animal lab. We would anesthetize the goats and then shoot them in their legs, and then the medics would be taught to treat the wounds to prevent infection. The only place we ever shot a goat was in the soft tissue of the leg because the medics were only trained to treat wounds to the extremities. What bothered me the most is that I had very little to do. The sergeants did the teaching and I did the paperwork. It was very discouraging. The closest I got to a knife was working my rotation in the emergency room, but there were very few real emergencies. The typical case seemed to be a soldier with a chronic back problem.

Julie, our second daughter, was born at Fort Bragg. Her birth was the highlight of our stay there. Kay's bag of waters broke around eight o'clock, just before it was time for me to leave for work one morning. I figured it would be hours before the baby was born, so I took my surgical texts along for the long hours of labor. We arrived at the hospital around 8:45 A.M. The friendly gynecologist, also anticipating hours of labor, asked, "Why don't you come have breakfast with me? And then we'll go back." We'd just filled our trays when he got a stat call. He answered. It was Kay—she was

44

ready. We rushed up to the delivery room, barely making it in time as Julie was born. My breakfast went untouched, and I never cracked a medical book. But Julie was another beautiful daughter, and it sure was nice not having to wait the twenty-two hours of labor that Dawn put us through.

I made sixteen more jumps, but my days in the army quickly became tedious. I was anxious to move on, to begin practicing real medicine again. I had a lot of time on my hands, a lot of time to think about what I wanted to do with my life. The challenge of cardiovascular surgery seemed most appealing, but the decision to continue training after my discharge from the army was not an easy one to make. Many questions needed to be answered—first and foremost, should I put my family, particularly Kay, through this? Another move. More study. More time away from family activities. More stress, more expenses, and less pay for another two years. I was already thirty-three years old and not in practice yet. I'd be thirty-five before I would be out developing a practice. On the other hand, I felt I needed the training to exercise the atrophied portion of my brain that had taken care of patients. I didn't feel I had lost my surgical skills, but the process of evaluating and caring for a patient, the decision-making process, seemed to be a faint gray memory.

What should I do? I was still a general surgeon and could easily go into practice somewhere and provide for my family. But my inner feeling of wanting to better myself, of wanting to do more, wouldn't go away. For months, the tug-of-war continued. Kay and I talked it over—over and over again. She was soothing and supportive, but we both knew that the decision was mine.

To make the decision more difficult, Dr. Louis

Rodgers, a close friend and general surgeon back in Des Moines, Iowa, called. He said he knew I would be leaving the army in a year or so, and he wanted me to consider returning to Des Moines to practice with him and two other fine surgeons.

Pressure began to mount for a decision. While Dr. Rodgers's offer was in the back of my mind, I began to look at cardiac programs. The desire to be in an operating room, touching human hearts, was still in the back of my mind. The closest and most logical was a program in Charlotte, North Carolina, a very busy program with lots of vascular surgery (surgery on blood vessels of the lungs and abdomen and to the brain) plus a mammoth amount of cardiac surgery on adults, but very little on children. It was a high-profile program with a very good reputation. Twenty-six surgeons had already applied for the program's one residency slot. I felt I had very little chance but was encouraged by Kay to take a look at it.

"It's only ninety minutes away. What can you lose?" she asked.

So off to Charlotte I went. My visit at Charlotte Memorial was a combination of pleasant southern hospitality and a frank interview with Dr. Robichek, the chief of cardiac surgery. I watched an impressive display of quick, efficient surgery by Dr. Robichek, who started and finished a carotid endarterectomy (cleaning out an artery in the neck that feeds the brain) in a matter of thirty minutes when most surgeons take three times as long.

I also had a candid discussion with one of the residents. He said he liked the program, but he had very little time to do any sleeping. He'd lost weight. He looked fatigued. He looked like he had been in a concentration camp. He didn't seem entirely satisfied and looked as if he was just hoping to last long enough to finish the training and acquire his thoracic surgery board certificate. It made me uncomfortable. It made me hesitate and vacillate.

I thought on my drive back home to Fayetteville that the residency would be a good one. But something troubled me. It seemed that the residents got stuck with a lot of routine work. Plus, they were so overloaded with patients, they had little time for reading and studying. But what troubled me the most was that I'd still be far from my real home in the Midwest. I began to realize how much family ties meant to both Kay and me, how much we both felt that our children needed to see their grandparents.

A day after I returned to Fayetteville, Dr. Francis Robichek called to tell me that the position was mine if I wanted it. I couldn't believe it. Two dozen other applicants were panting for the position, possibly waiting for months for a call, and here I received an offer within a day. Was the call for real, or was it just a dream? I really didn't know! I reached down and pinched my butt during the phone call just to be sure. The pain was real. Yes, I was awake, and Dr. Robichek was at the other end of the line, offering me the position in his kind Eastern European accent. I was listening, wishing I had already made up my mind to say yes, but I knew I had to tell him I couldn't give him an immediate answer. I told him I had already decided to look at another residency program, but I was almost certain that I would accept his offer. Actually, I didn't think I would have a choice. I thought Dr. Carl Almond at the University of Missouri was just being kind in accepting me for a visit to his program. Deep down, I knew I was not university material, and I had done my post-graduate training at a private hospital, not at a university. I told Dr. Robichek that I would have an answer for him in a week, and he said that was fine.

On the plane ride to Missouri, the clouds drifting by seemed to me like missed opportunities. I thought to myself, *I want to make sure this Missouri program is not a missed cloud drifting by.* It was close to home, which for me was like giving it a quarter-mile head start in a one-mile race. As the plane moved west, the decision seemed to take a life of its own and fill my body. I knew where I belonged. I felt I was going home.

The plane landed, and there he stood: Carl Almond, my chief-to-be. Standing only five feet six, he was as thick as he was wide, a burly man with tree-stump legs representing stability—a smile on his broad, affable face and a friendly voice exuding comfort and confidence the instant I shook his hand. He immediately impressed me with his easygoing nature. Little did I know that Carl Almond, C.A., was known not so fondly as "big C, little a," Ca, the medical symbol for cancer, because of his malignant nature in the operating room.

As we engaged in small talk from the airport to the university, I knew I had already been overcome by emotion. Objectivity was no longer a factor. I hoped I would be offered the position, even before we arrived at the hospital. I wanted to come to Missouri.

Make me an offer, I thought to myself. *I'll just say yes, and save everybody a lot of time.*

I tried to suppress my elation. I knew I should remain sober, that I shouldn't show too much eagerness, that I should play hard to get. I must have performed well. I found out two years later from a surgeon friend that Dr. Almond thought I had been much too formal. He confided with my surgeon friend that I hadn't smiled much and that I was almost "army-like," answering many of his questions with a "sir" on the end.

At his office, Dr. Almond immediately summoned the residents to take me on a tour of the facility. He introduced three residents—one from Mexico, one from India, and one from Argentina. No Americans. Strange, I thought. But then it dawned on me. Missouri must not be considered a top-notch residency program high on the list of American applicants. I chose to ignore this. I just wanted a residency close to home. Come hell or high water, good residency or bad, I wanted to work here.

The residents were pleasant, talkative, and enthusiastic during my tour of the hospital, taking two to three hours of their time showing me their patients and the surgeries they had performed. It seemed like a good variety of cases. They said they liked the program, and they described the chief as a tough boss whom they had grown to respect, perhaps even fear. Their anxiety seemed as clear to me as artificial snow in a crystal ball, but I wasn't ruffled. I figured I could put up with anything for two years.

After the tour, I walked back to my hotel to reflect, to refine my thinking, and to get ready for a night of entertainment at the chief's home. I was picked up by Dr. Almond, anticipating a night in an elegant home. I wasn't prepared for what I saw as we entered his drive. The house, which must have been ninety years old, was a trashy place in one of Columbia's worst neighborhoods. The siding was falling off, many windows were boarded, there were holes in the screens, and the house crouched behind a jungle of tangled bushes and vines, which was probably just as well since the house looked so terrible. I hoped the house didn't reflect the quality of Dr. Almond's surgical program—or his surgical success.

The steps to the door were slanted and loose, creating a precarious entry. I couldn't believe it! A cardiac surgeon living in this? I didn't know whether to laugh or cry. I couldn't wait to see inside. Almond opened the screen door carefully because the hinges were loose, and we entered a kitchen cluttered with pots and pans and an aroma so exquisite I forgot my surroundings. There were two young children and Dr. Almond's lovely wife, a charming, attractive woman with an aristocratic air. If she resented her surroundings, it never showed. The chief's wife and the nanny, a short, rotund black woman, were preparing the food while we stood around in the small, humid, unkept kitchen filled with delicious smells, munching on marinated dove breasts and quail thighs fried in some kind of butter and spice sauce.

Wow! This guy knows how to live, I thought. *Who needs an ostentatious house when food like this makes you forget where you are?*

The visit was delightful. I felt at home. It was like being in a farmhouse at harvest time. Warm. Soothing. Satisfying. With the appetizers gone, we were ushered into the dining room, where a large, elegant table set with fine china and silver stood on an old, sagging floor. First expensive champagne, and then dinner was served—a Caesar salad so large it was enough for a meal by itself, then a tasty entree of twice-baked potatoes and filet of sole stuffed with crabmeat and smothered in cream and cheese sauce. This was heaven! This was an expensive dinner. This was a snow job. I knew with certainty that he wanted me as a resident. And I knew I would not turn him down.

The decision was made right then and there. Any man who could live happily like this got my vote. I thought it was great that this big chief could feel so relaxed, comfortable, and satisfied living in such a dilapidated old home. I thought more of him for that than anything else.

I arrived home the next day with a broad smile on my face. Kay knew I had made up my mind before I uttered a word. We talked, and she was relieved that a decision had been made, although she later confided in me that she didn't realize what she was in for—sometimes going two or three days without seeing me and being cooped up with two little girls while being pregnant with our third daughter, Lori.

I applied for an early discharge and was accepted. I called Dr. Robichek in Charlotte and let him know my decision. He wasn't happy, but I don't think he was surprised. He had sensed that I wanted to be closer to home.

I called him eighteen years later for a young resident in the general surgery program at Iowa Methodist who was looking for a cardiac training program. Surprisingly, he hadn't forgotten me. "Oh yes! You're the one who turned me down!" he exclaimed. What could I say?

My last day in the army, a sergeant at the discharge post told me I couldn't leave because the commander of the base had rescinded all early terminal leaves prior to discharges. What the sergeant and I didn't know was that the commander's order applied to everyone except physicians. I glared at the sergeant and told him he

51

could stuff the commander's orders up his rectum! I was really hacked. He could try to stop me, I told him, but I was leaving for my residency. I told him to send my discharge papers to Missouri and I would sign them there in two weeks when I was officially out of the army. I turned to walk out the door, with the sergeant yelling, "You can't do that! You can't do that!"

"Oh yeah? Just watch."

I strode out the door and jumped in the car with Kay and the girls without looking back. I half expected to see a military police car pursuing us and half expected to be picked up and arrested for being AWOL (absent without leave), but my anger had overcome my good sense and fear. Two days later, a lieutenant called and told me the army had made a mistake. I would be getting my papers in a few days.

Back in Training

As the center line zipped by, my thoughts turned to questions and doubt. Had I made the right decision? Was I really capable? Did I want it badly enough? Over and over again, as the miles went by, the same nagging questions returned, only to be interrupted by the cries of our one-year-old, Julie, and the attention-seeking screams of her older sister, Dawn. Kay seemed to tolerate the noise and confusion better than I did, but even she was anxious about our move to Missouri. The small Volvo station wagon was far from spacious, jammed to the ceiling with stuff, allowing little room for two adults, two children, a German shepherd, and a stray cat that had adopted our family.

I was anxious to start, to see the chief and the other residents. Even more, I was eagerly anticipating learning something new. Would it be as exciting as I expected? Would it be a letdown? Or, even worse, would I let them down by not measuring up?

Within the first hour of our arrival in Columbia, I called Dr. Almond, letting him know we had arrived. He seemed friendly and eager to see me again. A meeting was scheduled for the next day, even though I had a week before I needed to be at the hospital—a week to clean and move into the house we had purchased three months before. A week to settle in. We thought.

Imagine our shock, exasperation, disappointment, and discouragement the next day when Kay and I learned that there had been a change in plans. After driving halfway across the country, we would have to pick up again, for the chief had decided that I should start my training 200 miles southwest, at the state chest hospital. We had thought my training would last two years—a full year in Columbia followed by a year at the chest hospital in Mount Vernon. But no, he needed me in Mount Vernon for six months, followed by a year in Columbia, and then back to Mount Vernon for the final six months. That meant three moves in two years instead of one! I was so pissed I could barely think or see straight, but I managed to keep my composure and hold my temper in Dr. Almond's presence. In fact, I even managed a semblance of enthusiasm.

At least he gave us some more time to get organized for our unexpected move. A good thing, too, because the house we had bought wasn't ready for us. The previous owners wanted one more day to move out.

Then came another irritation. The van hauling our household belongings had broken down somewhere in the mountains in Tennessee. They had no idea how long it would take to fix it. As it turned out, it came two and a half weeks later, and maybe that was a blessing in disguise because later that day we went to our newly purchased home and, wow! What a mess!

It's amazing all the things we missed when we decided to buy the house. They were all too obvious now that the house was empty. The cupboards were layered with years of grease. The carpets, which initially looked just dirty, turned out to be rotting from spilled food and pet pee. The walls were impregnated with dirt and marked by crayons, boot heels, and scratches. Shingles were missing from the roof. Four windows were cracked or broken, and most were not sealed. And everything, inside and out, needed paint.

How had we missed so much? How could we have been so blind? Had we been that anxious to move? Apparently so. Too late to do anything about it now, so we just shrugged and went to work. We had two to three weeks to work on the house—but no furniture. Fortunately, we had brought our sleeping bags, so we managed to "camp out" in our battered, dirty new home, happy to be together and knowing one day we would be able to laugh at the whole experience.

Finally, after more than two weeks of cleaning, painting, and repairing, our van arrived. I'm sure the chief wondered if I would ever show up for training, and I had begun to wonder myself. I was ready to go.

Kay and I spent many nights laboring through the early-morning hours, unpacking and repacking, trying to decide what to take to Mount Vernon and what to leave behind for our temporary renters who would enjoy our reconditioned house for the next six months.

Finally, on a hot, humid morning we loaded the last few items into a U-Haul. I pulled into the street, then stopped and waited for Kay to pass me in the Volvo. She would lead the way. Nothing happened. No Kay. I waited, thinking any second now she'll pull in front of me. *No Kay. No Volvo.* I knew she had been ready. I knew she was about to start the wagon. I pushed the truck door open with disgust, incensed that nothing was moving. As I rounded the corner of the back of the truck, there was the answer! The Volvo was listing badly, with its back wheel hanging free in a shallow ditch by the driveway. Kay was going nowhere. As she saw me coming around the truck, huffing, puffing, and fuming with impatience, all she could do was burst out laughing. She was too frustrated and tired to cry, or to worry about what I might say. I dropped to the lawn next to the Volvo, my elbows on my thighs to prop up my chin. I stared at the wheel and listened to Kay's penetrating laughter in disbelief. Then I burst out laughing. And we laughed—harder and harder. Nothing else would have salvaged the moment.

After a wrecker resurrected the Volvo, we were under way. I told Kay to follow me. If you need to stop, I said, just honk the horn. Off we went—me in the noisy truck with the German shepherd, Kay in the Volvo with our two little girls and a nervous cat with sharp claws.

After a hundred miles or so, Kay couldn't take it anymore. She leaned on the horn. Nothing. I just kept going, oblivious to the turmoil behind me. I couldn't hear the horn, and Kay couldn't understand why I refused to stop. So she leaned on the horn some more. The longer she waited and the more she honked, the louder the kids cried. The crying and honking made the cat even more nervous, and for what must have been the fifteenth time, it jumped onto her shoulder, digging its claws into her skin.

The Volvo sped by. I had no doubt, reading Kay's lips as she leaned toward the passenger side of the car, that it was time to stop. Time for a break. Why hadn't she just honked? I wondered. Why all this fuss, rage, and bother? I knew enough to hold my tongue. Dawn was hungry. Julie's pants were full. And the cat had some of Kay's skin. I was about to get the chewing out of my life. My pleasant, oblivious ride in the truck had come to an abrupt, tongue-lashing end. And we were only halfway there. All I could do in reply to her rage was say, "Sorry, I couldn't hear the horn." All that, just to get to a dirty little cottage infested with cockroaches, ants, cobwebs, and more greasy cupboards. More work for Kay.

Mount Vernon was a quiet, clean little town of 1,100 in the southwest corner of Missouri. It reminded me of the town I grew up in. The people were friendly. Many worked at the State Chest Hospital. New doctors were welcomed with open hospitality. Kay and I made many friends, but I had little time for socializing.

The hospital had been a tuberculosis sanitarium, very busy, twenty years earlier. It was now fighting for survival, trying to change to survive. The name and mission had been changed—to take care of any indigent patient with any kind of chest disease or condition. Many were extremely poor, had never been to a doctor, and their nutrition and hygiene in many cases eroded their human existence.

The senior resident had already been there six months. Now, he was in charge and had first choice of the surgery cases. He was kind, intelligent, and reassuring. Also, I later learned that he was compulsively neat and at the far end of the bell-shaped curve in terms of being insecure about his surgery. He coped by taking things slowly, methodically, and cautiously. Fine for him, perhaps, but frustrating for me. Nevertheless, I told myself, *If he's fair, I will stand by his side no matter what.*

The first test came in the operating room. The chief resident was the lead surgeon. The staff surgeon was his first assistant, and I was the scissors man, the second assistant who just stands there, holding retractors if required and cutting sutures after they're tied. That would have been all right, but the routine case, requiring the partial removal of a lung, took five hours. I bit my tongue every fifteen minutes. His moves were slow, careful, and cautious. I felt like I was watching a chess game. I'd assisted in similar surgeries during my general surgical training, and I wasn't accustomed to this pace. An operation like this, in my experience, should take less than two hours. I watched and wondered, but said nothing.

Four weeks went by. Surgery continued at the same slow pace, elevating my impatience. The fact that I hadn't performed a surgery, or even assisted, irritated my frustration like a growing, ripening pimple. I tried to vent steam at home, but was cut short by Kay.

"Look," she said, "you have been here only four weeks. You wanted to do this. You are here, so we'll stick it out and finish it. If you don't, you'll always be frustrated, and you'll always wonder what might have been."

The staff surgeon, a brilliant young Mexican native with good technique and lots of patience, approached me the next morning. He and the senior resident thought it was time for me to start doing surgeries—at least the easy ones. What a pleasant surprise! The way the first four weeks had gone, I really hadn't expected to do any surgery for at least two more months.

My first surgery was a sixty-year-old man, a heavy smoker with an ugly spot on his right lung. It looked very much like a cancer, but we couldn't prove it ahead of time. He needed his chest opened. He agreed.

I could hardly wait, but the surgery was scheduled for the next day. I went home, feeling I could perform the surgery but not certain that I knew everything I needed to know. I assumed I would be peppered with questions while I performed the surgery. I wanted to be ready. I hit the books, reviewing anatomy, physiology, and complications. I knew I was ready. *Were they?* I wondered, as my head hit the pillow.

I awoke before the alarm the next morning. As I

58

walked to the hospital, just across the grounds from the cluster of cottages, I nearly broke into a run. The urge to start the surgery had me champing at the bit like a horse caged at the starting gate. "Calm down!" I said to myself. "Look and act cool and calculating like an erudite surgeon."

Rounds were the first chore of the morning—paying visits to patients who had already had surgery or were awaiting surgery. Most were not awake at 6:00 A.M. It was a boring and laborious chore—necessary, an important part of surgery—but today my mind was in the O.R. (operating room), not on the early-morning rounds. The chief resident noticed but didn't say anything. He, of all persons, understood quite well, having gone through the same thing just six months earlier. This was my first major surgery in a new program. Damn right! I was overly concerned.

As the patient was placed on the table, prepared and anesthetized, I kept telling myself I was ready. Yet, internally, minute seeds of doubt and hesitation sprouted and grew.

The patient was cleaned with an antiseptic and then draped, ready for the first incision. With a deep breath, I looked at the clock as the knife was slapped into my palm: 8:00 A.M. sharp. I wanted to be done by eleven o'clock.

Here goes. Instinctively, from my general surgery training, I drove the knife hard and deep into the skin and flesh. The cut needed to be curved and clean, without hesitation. This would prevent too much tissue from being traumatized and would help with the healing. I hadn't forgotten that principle, I told myself for reassurance.

As the cut was made quickly, with authority, the

other two surgeons gasped. My technique was too fast. Slow down. Too much bleeding, they mumbled nervously. They wanted more caution. More time. A wound dried by lots of cauterization. *And dead, too,* I thought, accepting their critique.

Finally, forty-five minutes later, we were inside the chest. I had seen other surgeons accomplish the same in ten minutes, and that's how I wanted to work. After moving the lung downward to grasp the upper lobe, I could feel the huge mass. It felt bad. Cancer for sure. Then the barrage of piercing, thought-provoking, needling questions began. I didn't know the answers to all of them, but I did to most. I wondered if they were asking questions to relieve the tension. They seemed edgy and uneasy, shifting their weight from one leg to the other. As I started to expose the structure near the center of the lung, their heads and hands were constantly in the way. They seemed to apply the verbal brakes as I tried to proceed.

They must think I have no idea what to do, I thought. *Or at least they want to make sure I do know what to do.* I was irritated. To me, they seemed like nervous Nellies.

Looking back, I realize they had every right to be nervous because it was a delicate operation and they didn't know me or my abilities. The arteries in the lungs are soft, almost like butter and they're easily cut or damaged by sutures. Pull a little too tightly or move a little too quickly and there can be massive, uncontrollable bleeding. They had to protect the patient, and I should have realized and appreciated that.

My first task was to isolate, divide, and tie off the pulmonary artery branches to the upper part of the lung containing the mass. I had done this before with other surgeons, without complaints—in fact, with encouragement and compliments. I proceeded with too much speed and flash.

"*No, no, no, no!*" came the machine-gun fire.

The staff surgeon was uneasy. He took the instruments from my hands all too frequently to show me his way, doing most of the critical dissection. A "damn!" almost slipped from my lips as I saw the vessels slowly unfold. I tried to reach for the next instrument but had it snatched away as the boss on the other side of the table continued to show me. Hours seemed to pass, and they did. I looked up: 10;30 A.M. Not even half done. This was irritatingly unbelievable.

I'm not the surgeon for this case, I thought. *I'm the pseudosurgeon. Is this how I'm supposed to learn for the next two years?*

The surgery continued. I watched most of it, did maybe 30 percent. Was I happy? Hell, no! But I certainly was a good actor. Six hours. God! Way too long, I was certain, but had I missed something in my previous surgical training? Was this slow, deliberate, highly meticulous, and cautious way really how chest surgery should be done?

Within two weeks, I had a chance at another big case. This time, a patient with a large abdominal aortic aneurysm needed surgery. The large blood vessel passing through the abdomen had weakened and bulged in one spot like a partially inflated tubular balloon. The vessel was ready to rupture and needed repair right away, with a section of woven dacron tubing to replace the weakened portion. I had done the operation before in my general surgery training, taking less than two hours to complete it. A piece of cake. Fun, I thought. And I was charged up even more when the O.R. nurses asked me how long it would take. "Oh, not more than two hours," I replied with confidence.

Wrong again. Try five hours. From the moment I started the incision, it was a constant verbal hassle mixed with admonitions to slow down. Each stitch I inserted into the graft and the aorta was not quite right. Time after time, when I tried to speed the process, the two senior surgeons would scream in unison, "Look out! Don't do that! You'll get the patient in trouble." To make matters worse, the O.R. nurses jokingly ribbed me about the added three hours. They knew I was frustrated. But I was stuck—caught between my frustrating anger and Kay's admonition to stick it out.

I finally enjoyed a small measure of satisfaction during one of our most simple procedures—the insertion of a chest tube to drain a lung. I had been in residency only two months at the time but had performed the insertion many times during my general surgery residency. The senior resident didn't believe me. At first, he wanted me to go ahead and do it. Then he wanted to observe, to make sure I performed the procedure correctly. Finally, he just had to show me.

The sweet, gray-haired, very weak woman who needed the procedure couldn't breathe very well. An X ray showed that her entire chest cavity on the right side was filled with fluid. Her left breast had been removed years before. Now, we suspected that the cancer had spread to the lining of her chest, producing the fluid, collapsing her right lung, and making her very short of breath. If we inserted a tube into the chest cavity and drained the fluid, the lung should expand and her breathing should improve.

We planned to perform the procedure in her room. The tube was ready, local anesthetic was injected into

62

her skin and between her ribs, and I made a small incision in the skin just below and to the side of her right breast. For some reason, the chief resident wasn't sure I would do it correctly. He stopped me, slipped on a pair of sterile rubber gloves, and tactfully pushed me aside as he confidently stated, "Let me show you how I would like this done."

I stepped aside, half pissed and half surprised. I didn't think this was such a big deal, and I internally boiled, "Oh, man!" as I moved to the end of the bed.

He grabbed the tube with the end of a big clamp and pushed it through the incision between her ribs. "See? That's how I want it done." She squirmed from the pressure as the tube popped in. Out came some fluid. The resident picked up the end of the tube as he waited for the nurse to give him the end of the drainage tubing. It wasn't ready. So there he stood with the chest tube in hand, waiting, not realizing that he had the chest tube aimed right at himself. I saw my chance.

"Cough! Cough that fluid out!" I commanded.

She did. A solid stream of warm yellow juice jetted out, catching the chief resident right under his chin and running down the front of his white dress shirt and tie.

"That's right!" I encouraged. "Cough real hard!"

The next salvo hit him in the pants, and I was scrambling out the door. I grabbed my side in uncontrollable laughter as I rounded the corner. The chief resident said nothing. To my surprise, after he finished draining the lung, he came down the hall to the office where I was waiting. He laughed. Then I started laughing.

"You bastard, you got me!" he exclaimed. And we both laughed some more.

63

I was just beginning to get used to the slow, odd way of doing things in Mount Vernon when the six months had passed and it was time to pack and move back to Columbia. The trip back was uneventful, but my mind was busy. I knew the next year in Columbia would be much more intense, busy, and demanding. The chief resident and young staff surgeon in Mount Vernon had repeatedly alluded to the change of pace during my first six months there.

As I sat in the cab of the moving truck, bumping down the pavement with a monotonous rhythm, my thoughts turned to anticipation of what the university hospital setting might be like. I hadn't experienced that kind of environment since my medical school days, now nine years in the past.

As I recalled, the university hospital medical style was slow, rigid, cautious—mixed with numerous consultations and duplications, all in the name of education. Preop assessments, scheduling, and surgeries took much longer than in private practice. I was sure the University of Missouri would be no different. I dreaded having to suppress my impatience and my disdain for the formality I would have to conform to. I knew it would be hard for me not to blow up, at least internally. I knew I would not be very happy in the coming year. I could only look forward to its end, hoping to learn something in the process.

I reflected back as the truck rolled on, realizing what I had learned from my experience in Mount Vernon. Despite my frustrations, I had learned one thing from these slow, deliberate men, and that was to follow patients carefully and conscientiously after an operation, to maintain an intense vigil of postoperative care. I hadn't acquired this attitude with such intensity

64

during my general surgical training. I hadn't appreciated it at the time, but the two young surgeons in Mount Vernon were so conscientious and kind to their patients that it had rubbed off.

Their intense attention to care after surgery had saved many patients from unfortunate complications and, in a few cases, even death. Their attitude also taught me to care intensely about my patients—not just before and during surgery, but after surgery as well.

I recalled that three months into my residency in Mount Vernon, I was assigned the case of a sixty-year-old woman with diffuse disease preventing the exchange of oxygen in both lungs. She was slowly suffocating to death. We hoped there might be a medicine that could reverse the process, but we had to explore that possibility with a biopsy, using a small incision to remove a small piece of lung to be studied under a microscope for accurate diagnosis. The woman, blue and short of breath despite her mask for oxygen, reluctantly agreed to the biopsy, not convinced when I made it sound easy. I didn't appreciate the risk such a routine procedure could be for a woman in her grave condition. I was still inexperienced and optimistic. It was just a little incision that wouldn't hurt at all. And yet for her it was a huge, traumatic operation. I didn't realize that for someone with lungs as poor as hers, even a small incision could be deadly.

The surgery went well, but afterwards her condition worsened. She became dependent on a ventilator. I tried in vain for the next two weeks to save her. My feelings of guilt grew because I had told her there was little risk. My postoperative care intensified. She could not die! She did.

I went back to the drab consultation room to tell her family. They knew she was dying. They were prepared. I wasn't. As I told them she was gone, my voice tightened and I began to cry. I broke apart with tears, and the family wrapped me in their arms. Was I feeling sorry for myself? Was I feeling guilt or empathy? Or had the two young surgeons who I thought were slow, insecure, and overly cautious taught me to care that much? Months later, I was sure they had, but I never admitted it to them.

As the truck rolled on, my thoughts turned back to Columbia and the chief of the program. Dr. Carl Almond. What is he really like? Is he really the malignant terror many say he is? Is he fair? Will he be a good teacher? Will he allow me to do a good share of the cardiac surgery? On and on, the questions repeated themselves.

My anxiety grew as we neared Columbia—not so much because of the slow, regimented pace of university hospital life, or even the prospect of working under a terror chief surgeon. I believed I could handle that, and I truly believed that a good deal of it was just a show to make a point. What I really dreaded were the long, intense hours that would sap my energy and my joy for life. I would like to preserve that during the coming year, but I knew I wouldn't be able to. As it turned out, it was worse than I expected—not twelve-hour days but twenty-hour days, not sixty-minute hours but eighty-minute hours.

I also dreaded rotating back with the chief resident, who was moving back from Mount Vernon to Columbia at the same time I was. Dr. Show-me-how-to-put-the-test-tube-in, Dr. Compulsive, Dr. Slow, Dr. Insecure would need lots of support for the next six months while he was finishing his senior residency. I knew it wouldn't be easy, yet I knew I would have to help him as much as possible for both of us to survive. I liked the man. He was pleasant, honest, patient, a genuinely good person. I just hated how much time he took to do everything. I swore to myself that I would give him my support, but I knew it would be trying. I think he must have felt the same way about me. We could sense that we didn't like each other's style, but we knew we needed each other.

I mulled this over and over as the truck rolled into Columbia. We were unloaded by 11:00 P.M., the boxes piled high. I would have no time to help Kay unpack. Dr. Almond wanted rounds finished by 7:30 A.M., and he wanted to meet at eight o'clock sharp. That meant I needed to be up by 5:00 A.M. and out of the house by 6:00, leaving Kay with two small children, a dirty house, and piles of unpacked boxes. She was not a happy camper.

The 5:00 A.M. alarm went off. I threw back the covers and jumped to my feet. I wanted to get started, to see how bad it would be. Most of all, I wanted to finish this residency and begin practicing surgery. I knew the year would be grinding, like a barefooted marathon run.

The first morning of rounds were just as bad as I feared. Only eight patients, and yet it took ninety minutes. "We have to know everything about these patients," the chief resident kept repeating. Dr. Almond met with us after rounds. He wanted to know "everything." *What a waste,* I kept telling myself. *What an impossibility. Oh, well, I'm going to hang in there, but this is going to be a hell of a long year.*

Surgery was scheduled for later that morning. I

can't for the life of me remember what it was, but I do remember one thing: I felt like a little piglet sucking hind tit. I was third assistant. Dr. Almond was the surgeon. A junior staff surgeon was first assistant. The chief resident was second assistant. And I was the absolute do-nothing person at the end of the table.

It quickly became apparent that Dr. Almond could be mild and pleasant one moment and a terror the next, particularly in the operating room. His "big C, little a" nickname fit. I don't know if he knew of the nickname, but if he did, he probably was proud of it. His favorite saying was, "I don't get ulcers, I give ulcers."

Almond never seemed to be satisfied, even when things were going well. I was there as third assistant to learn how he wanted things done, but all I seemed to learn was how to duck, or at least tolerate, verbal bullets that seemed to ricochet around the room, most of them aimed at the first and second assistants. He wasn't harsh to me at first because I was new. As a junior resident, you just kind of stood by and chuckled, watching the senior resident try to satisfy the tyrant. Still, the anticipation, seeing a thirty-two-year-old man being chewed out like a five-year-old and knowing my time would come, was a bit unsettling. I was dreading my turn six months later, when I would be first or second assistant.

Heart surgery during my training frequently took all day. Long heart surgeries were common everywhere back then. The heart-lung machines were not as good as they are today, and we didn't have the cooling solutions to preserve the heart as well as we do today. Putting a new heart valve in might take two or three hours, but then there would be a long weaning process, waiting for the heart to recover from the shock of surgery. We'd sit there, sometimes for hours, trying to get the heart off of the artificial pump.

The first day was no exception. Finally, at 4:00 P.M., six hours after we started, we moved the patient into the intensive care unit. The surgery was a success, but the day wasn't over. I had more rounds and the new postop patient to care for. I thought, since I was not on call the first night, that I would be home by 7:00 P.M. Wrong. Everything dragged on. Afternoon rounds were three hours. I felt they could have been done in one. The chief resident wanted a complete report on the new admission. And on and on. Finally, at 10:00 P.M., I was fed up and said, "Hey, I'm going home. See you tomorrow." The chief resident seemed stunned, but I didn't give a damn. I soon learned that a 10:00 P.M. departure would be early, even for days when I was not on call.

I also discovered that in the operating room, as far as Dr. Almond was concerned, the chief surgeon was lord. Which meant he could yell, scream, rant, and rave. I wasn't accustomed to this. I didn't like it, and I wanted to poke at it if I ever had the chance.

Two months after my return to Columbia, I was assigned what I thought should be an easy case—a lobectomy, the removal of one half of a lung because of cancer. Dr. Almond wanted to assist me, even though the chief resident or a junior staff surgeon would normally assist in this kind of surgery. Prior to surgery, I wondered why. The answer came quickly. After the chest was opened, Dr. Almond let me start the dissection of lung vessels. Immediately, some bleeding started when one of the small branches was nicked—nothing serious. Dr. Almond saw his chance to take over, and as he did, he proceeded to ridicule, poke, and joke about my surgical technique. He grabbed the suction device and proceeded to do all the dissection, exposing the vessels for ligation in a couple of minutes while making cracks like "You're a high school Harry." "You operate like a cub scout." "Amateur hour, amateur hour." On and on he blasted, half pissing me off, half humiliating me. It couldn't have been a more unpleasant experience, yet with a good outcome for the patient. The surgery went efficiently fast.

At the time, I felt I wasn't given a chance to show my stuff, but later I realized there was a point Dr. Almond was trying to make. He was trying to keep me moving with confidence during surgery, to show me that you don't need to take all day to be a skilled, caring surgeon. Those revelations came later, however. At the time, all I could think of was the anger and humiliation. He'd called me a messy amateur. I wasn't used to that and felt I hadn't deserved it. If I had a chance to turn the tables, I would.

Two or three days later, Dr. Almond was performing a congenital heart repair on a three-year-old girl with a transposition of major vessels. He was in the midst of inserting a tube—surgeons call them cannulas—into the aorta when the cannula slipped and blood spurted all over the place until he put his finger over the hole. The place looked like a battlefield. I was standing by the anesthesiologist, observing, and my mouth just opened: "My god, what a mess! Amateur hour!"

The room suddenly grew quiet as Dr. Almond's eyes became two narrow silts. He pointed his finger at the door and said, "Out! Get out!" All of the other residents were slack-jawed. They couldn't believe I had spoken my mind. And neither could I. Nobody ever said such things to the chief!

The little girl didn't make it through surgery, although the inadvertent bleeding wasn't the cause. Her heart just wouldn't take over after surgery. The chief surgeon never spoke to me about my outburst. He just left me to steam, smolder, and wonder.

Unfortunately, for me, I paid the price for my verbal outburst again and again. It seemed I couldn't do anything right. I remember one night, a stabbing victim arrived at the emergency room. He'd been stabbed in the left chest, and it appeared he might be bleeding from the heart into the sac around it, putting pressure on the heart and causing it to labor, producing shock. Everybody seemed to be standing around, looking at this guy, doing nothing, letting him die right there in the emergency room. So I decided to open him up right then and there. I stopped the bleeding. It was from the lung and not his heart. We saved his life, even though I had misdiagnosed the source of the bleeding.

I was proud of my performance, but when I presented the case to a roomful of 130 residents, students, and staff surgeons, ol' Ca tore me apart: "You should have taken him to the operating room instead of playing the hero in the emergency room! It's much cleaner there! Less chance of infection! There was time!" You should have done this! You should have done that! On and on went the humiliating tirade in front of other residents and students. I stood there stunned. I just kind of ate it, feeling angry, wronged, and humiliated. To me, what I had done made sense because I had saved the patient's life, but to the chief I had been wrong because I had performed surgery outside the operating room. I didn't appreciate his tirade at the time, but he was really teaching me to think about the consequences of my decisions. In this case, I believe I made the right decision. The man healed without infection and left the hospital in five days.

Not long after that episode, another man was rushed into the emergency room while I was there. Chest X rays indicated massive bleeding into the chest cavity. It appeared his aorta was rupturing. I felt he needed a chest tube to drain the blood and relieve the pressure on his heart. As the tube was inserted, he struggled under the pain. As he did, the aorta must have ruptured completely. He moaned, passed out, and suddenly there was no blood pressure. As he sank, I had the sinking feeling he was dying before my eyes. He was in shock, as pale as the sheets—delirious, confused, in trouble. There was no time. I needed to retrieve him. I needed to *do something.*

I inserted a breathing tube into his throat and then rolled him onto his side and slashed his chest open with a scalpel. Can you imagine a chest full of blood— all of his blood? As I opened him up, the blood welled up and boiled all over us, all over our clothes, our shoes, the floors. It was a flood. It was frightening. And I felt that everyone was staring at me—the nurses, the janitor, the X-ray technician, the other residents. I knew it was too late. He died right there. So there I stood, my hand in the man's chest and around the bleeding aorta, blood everywhere, when Dr. Almond walked into the emergency room. He looked, and all he could say was, "Don't you ever learn?" And turned and walked away. That's the last I heard about that case.

Dr. Almond's presence was so intimidating, he presented such an aura of command and fear, that you almost wanted to flee or hide when you saw him coming into an operating room. Yet away from the O.R. atmosphere, he could be the friendliest person you would ever hope to meet. He was so proud once you'd made it through your residency. You were "his" resident. And I still catch myself using some of his favorite aphorisms, but in a kidding sort of way, when working with students or green surgeons: "What is this, amateur hour?" "You're operating like a high school Harry." "Stop masturbating the tissue."

His loyalty notwithstanding, I never came to agree with what I thought were harsh teaching methods. Also, I didn't agree with some of his surgical techniques, particularly his aortic valve operations. His methods in this case were too slow, too careful. He didn't move along the way he did in lung operations. It seemed to me that he tried to be too accurate, too safe. For some reason, he was overly concerned about whether the valve was seated and stitched properly. His checking and rechecking took time. Too much time would pass, and the heart would die. It was just too much for the heart to take, especially in those days when you couldn't cool the heart and preserve it the way we do today. He must have known the valve operations were his shortcoming because he always ranted and raved and yelled at us to help him during those cases.

Why he was that way with valve cases, I don't know, because he was a master with congenital heart defect operations and with lung surgeries. His results in those cases were excellent, but I don't believe we saved a single aortic valve patient while I was there. We lost them all, as I recall, although there were only a half dozen or so. By the time I was finished as senior resident, the chief's aortic valve track record had become the object of constant gallows humor. We coped by joking: "Don't think of it as losing a patient but gaining a bed." It was "time" to gain another bed in the ward, "time" for a break from postop care. No late night on those days.

Dr. Almond wasted no time putting me into the pressure cooker once I became senior resident. Part of it was my fault, I suppose. I hadn't noticed that he had a fetish for wanting the senior resident in the operating room before the patient was put under with anesthetics. So of course, for my first case as senior resident, I arrived in my own good time, after the patient had been anesthetized. There the commander stood. His neck veins stuck out even farther than my father's. I thought his anger was ridiculous at the time. I thought he was way off base. But he made his point. He told me in no uncertain terms that you need to be with your heart patients as they're being anesthetized because it is a danger period during which you might need to open a patient quickly. Anything short of being there with the patient, as far as he was concerned, was abandonment.

There I stood again, a thirty-four-year-old man being hammered like I was a five-year-old. It sure would have been easier if he had just told me that ahead of time, but that wouldn't have made as much of an impression, and that was not his method. His method was shock. I must admit that I use the technique myself on occasion today, not with the intimidating intensity he employed, but more in a joking way, hoping to teach while breaking the tension at the same time.

About that same time, shortly after my senior residency began, the new junior resident arrived—a real character named T. E. Dye, known simply as Ted

74

Dye. He was the only resident during my time in Columbia whom even the chief avoided. Ol' Ca had enough sense to assign Ted to his assistant, apparently realizing that there was no way the two of them could function together. Later, I assumed the chief must have known about this character before he accepted him. But anyway, he apparently needed a body to fill the vacancy.

Ted had just come from another training program down south. He hadn't liked it down there, from what he told me, and had told his former chief to shove it. So there he was, in Columbia. I remember, when he walked through the door, I saw this man in a pink flowery shirt with lace on the cuffs and a purse on his shoulder. The first thing I thought was, "Is this some kind of a new nurse with a mustache?"

"Hello, aah'm Ted Dye. Aah'm the new resident," he drawled as we shook hands.

I wondered if this guy would be any help at all. I later discovered that, despite his appearance, he was very opinionated, volatile, and assertive. I also found that I could calm him down and keep him out of trouble. Quite often, I acted as the intermediary between Ted and the junior staff surgeon. And much to my surprise, I thought I learned more from Ted than he ever learned from me. He'd learned a lot in his previous training program. It hadn't been the greatest, he said, but at least a few of their aortic valve patients had survived surgery. So here he was, the junior resident, at times teaching me, the senior resident, what he had learned at his previous residency.

Ted and I hit it off from the start. We felt comfortable together, and we seemed to agree about patient care. We made our rounds swiftly, tracked down any

75

test results we needed, and divided chores, finishing much earlier than I had during the previous six months. The days were much shorter now—ten or twelve hours instead of sixteen or twenty. We became a highly efficient team, but we were still frustrated at times by Dr. Almond's demands, particularly in the operating room.

I'll never forget the day we were operating on an eleven-year-old girl. We couldn't wean her from the heart-lung machine. Ted and I offered our ideas, somewhat timidly and without authority I must admit, in part because of our fear of the chief and in part because we'd had no experience with her particular problem.

The girl had been diagnosed several days earlier with a very unusual congenital heart problem called Ebstein's anomaly. Her tricuspid valve (the valve between the right atrium and the right ventricle) was positioned low within the right ventricle instead of higher between the two chambers. The malposition caused the valve to flap back and forth and then leak backwards. The operation to correct the problem entails either a valve replacement or a repositioning of the valve, the latter being preferable.

This girl's tests and angiograms appeared to reveal a classic case, and yet something looked strange. No one gave it a second thought. The operation began without a hitch. The cannulas to drain the heart and perfuse the body were in place. I was proud when I finished my part. The heart-lung machine was started as the chief was scrubbing his hands, getting ready to gown and glove. Within seconds, the heart-lung machine failed. Nothing seemed to be going through the oxygenator. Was it plugged? The chief, seeing the sudden excitement and hearing the distress, rushed into the room, verbally blasting me for doing something wrong. I stepped aside, feeling awful, making room for this hulk of steaming hot humanity. I wondered if my residency would be terminated.

The heart had been drained and almost half of her blood volume was stuck in the heart-lung machine. It wouldn't come out.

"What in the hell is the problem?" the chief yelled in frustration.

The girl's blood pressure was close to zero. The chief squeezed her heart as an almost instant decision was made to change the oxygenator on the heart-lung machine. That took five minutes. The girl was in shock. The machine was turned on again. We all sighed in relief. It seemed to be working. Suddenly, the same thing happened again. No flow. Shock.

"God help us" was my reaction as I watched the chief ranting, raving, and sweating in frustration.

"What the hell is going on here?" was his repetitive question.

None of us knew. Another reluctant but rapid decision was made to change the oxygenator again. This time the clue hit us like an obvious blow to the head. A cluster of clear, grapelike jelly dropped out of the tube connected to the girl as the oxygenator was being changed. The girl had a myxoma, a benign tumor of the heart that can grow to an enormous size before causing any problems, perhaps even breaking free, causing problems like strokes or artery blockages to the bowels, legs, or lung vessels when it's on the right side of the heart. This girl had the tumor on the right side of her heart, and it had just plugged our oxygenator—twice.

Quickly, the drainage tubes were advanced into

77

the large vena cavas (the large veins draining blood into the heart), and tapes were placed around the large veins to act as a noose to prevent the pieces of tumor from being sucked into the heart-lung machine oxygenator.

Now we had control. Slowly, the blood pressure increased to normal levels as more blood was transfused into the circuit. With everything stabilized, the right atrium was opened. There it was—a jellylike mass of soft, clear grapes of various sizes, the whole thing the size of a grapefruit. We extracted it in pieces. The heart was closed and allowed to recover.

Then the trouble came. The lungs were ventilated, and the weaning process from the pump was attempted. No luck. The heart would not do the work. What was wrong now? More pump support was given. The chief was really sweating and strangely quiet. Again we tried. Again and again. No luck. No results. We were stuck on the pump. We tried drugs to stimulate the heart and dilate the arteries. Nothing worked. This beautiful child was dying.

Ted and I stared at each other but dared not look at the chief. The idea hit us both simultaneously as we mumbled to each other: Open the pulmonary artery. Maybe the tumor has plugged the artery to the lungs. By this time, the chief was overcome by a combination of resignation and depression. He vetoed the idea when we meekly suggested that he open the pulmonary artery to see if a broken piece of tumor had lodged there.

"The pieces would be too small" was his tired retort.

He refused, saying it was too late. Ted and I were exasperated. Our eyes met, reflecting our disbelief and our congruent thought: *What have we got to lose?*

By now, we had been in the operating room for nearly seven hours and had gained nothing. Dr. Almond tried to wean several more times, but the process didn't come close to success. The girl started bleeding out her lungs. The lungs got stiff, and we eventually gave up. Quit. Just like that. The room was suddenly deathly silent. No one talking. No machines humming. Nobody moved. Tears ran down the nurses' cheeks as the decision to quit was made. I held my tears, but my throat ached from holding them back. The child was gone.

The chief had to face the family. I couldn't and didn't. I knew I would have broken down. Ted was silent. This little girl was the same age as his. He didn't say anything until two days later. By then an autopsy had been completed, showing a massive amount of broken tumor plugging the main pulmonary arteries. The pathologist wondered if the pieces could have been extracted. So did Ted and I. The chief was silent. He was not his confident, robust, boisterous self for weeks. Losing the child had hit him hard. The depression and devastation were on his face, but that didn't matter to Ted and me. Between ourselves, we remained highly critical and blamed the chief for not opening the pulmonary artery. We felt it was the girl's last chance. In our brash young ignorance, we knew we were right.

I thought I had learned a lot, working and trading ideas with Ted. Still, after more than three months as chief resident, I had not performed any cardiac surgery. The resident ahead of me, who was not very adept technically, never was given a chance to do any cardiac cases, and I was beginning to think I would go through my entire residency without any real training, eventually emerging as a pseudocardiac surgeon.

Fortunately, Dr. Almond left for two months, leaving the junior staff man in charge. Bypass surgery was fairly new at the time. I had seen very few. However, the junior staff man had gained considerable experience in bypass techniques during a fellowship with Dr. Denton Cooley in Texas. We performed twelve bypass operations while the chief was gone. All survived. That was the bulk of my bypass surgery training in my residency, but it was enough to give me the lift and confidence I needed.

After Dr. Almond returned, to my surprise, he helped me do some congenital heart repairs. The easy ones. He also taught me how to replace some mitral valves. Yet he would always be there, ranting and raving: "Watch out!" "Don't do that!" He had us do things in the name of "safety" to the point of inhibiting "speed," which is an essential ingredient of heart surgery, even today. Yet he wanted speed. I could tell he was frustrated with himself at times because of the lack of speed.

The chief did the difficult congenital cases with good success, then left the patients to us for postop care. We stayed with the children after the surgery day and night, sometimes going without sleep for two or three nights.

Were all training programs like the one I went through? I don't know, but I do know that many surgeons in training at that time had similar experiences. Many have told me they performed very little surgery, even under direct supervision. I hope and believe that it is different today. The tension and nervousness I encountered was a phenomenon of the time. Heart surgery was new in the early 1970s, especially for the senior staff surgeons who were veterans

80

in their fifties and sixties by the time these heart surgery procedures became prevalent. Many mistakes had been made, and they had made them. They were the experimenters and pioneers. It was no wonder they were cautious, something we younger surgeons couldn't relate to or appreciate. They tried to teach us to avoid the mistakes they had made while seeking better, safer techniques. And in fact, they couldn't teach us many of the techniques we use today because they hadn't been developed and didn't exist as they do today.

Politics and Paradox

The path to success as a heart surgeon is littered with political land mines. As the end of my training in Missouri approached, I thought I was pretty seasoned. I had a demanding internship, an intense surgical residency, Special Forces army service, and most of my cardiac residency under my belt. Now, to face the "real" world—in this case another young heart surgeon looking for an even younger surgeon to hire with a chance to become a full partner in two or three years. No guarantees, but it seemed like the perfect setup, a chance to join a successful practice in a Midwestern city near our families. We viewed the city as a place to settle down, a place to end our vagabond, transient existence, the place where we would anchor our lives. Just six months to go, and we could end our moves and I could begin practicing surgery! Six months back at the chest hospital in Mount Vernon.

Our third daughter, Lori, was born a month prior to our move back to the small town. Kay's labor was induced just after Thanksgiving so she could have the baby at the hospital in Columbia before our late December trip back to Mount Vernon. I remember that when we learned Kay was pregnant for the third time, we were both apprehensive, especially Kay. She wondered, sometimes with sobs, how she would be able to handle two small girls and a baby through two more moves—the one to Mount Vernon and then to my practice. She would sob, and I'd say, "Don't worry. I'll help." And she'd say, "Yeah, like you've helped in the past? You're always gone." Kay was in the hospital for just two days, and I couldn't believe how tough she was. She had planned ahead and had packed most of our belongings before Lori was born. Just a few days after Lori was born, we went out for a late Thanksgiving dinner—all five of us in a restaurant together, one big happy family. Kay handled it with aplomb.

The last six months at the chest hospital were pleasant and easy. Ted and I were the residents, and the junior staff surgeon was easy to work with. It was like a different place. Ted and I worked quickly, confidently, and easily. We'd finish our work early, make our rounds, and have time for a couple hours of tennis on the hospital courts before heading home. We even had time to study for our thoracic board examinations without staying up all night. We passed the tests, much to the relief of both of us. Kay enjoyed the six months, too. She was comfortable because I was relaxed and easier to live with.

Refreshed, in high spirits, and confident, we left Mount Vernon in late June and headed for our new home. We bought a house, thinking we would stay forever, and I arrived at the hospital loaded for bear, ready to take on patients and perform surgeries. Within weeks, however, it became apparent that I had made a bad choice. My style clashed with my employer's style. He seemed loud, noisy, and too fast in the operating room, even for me. He took big bites with the needle in very small arteries, and he always seemed to be in a rush. I can't criticize his techniques because he had a successful practice with an excellent track record. But as I saw it then and still see it today, a cardiac surgeon needs to move along, but he also needs to take his time with certain details that can prevent complications and sometimes make the difference between life and death. Making clean cuts, taking fine stitches, watching for loose plaque. These and other time-consuming details add up and make a difference.

To my dismay and most disconcertingly, I wasn't given a chance to perform many surgeries. The surgeon I had tied my future to had started the heart program at this particular hospital and had developed a close relationship with the cardiologist there. They were friends, and they seemed to have a close bond that prevented the surgeon from turning over cases to me, the newcomer. The cardiologist apparently didn't *want* his patients referred to someone he didn't know, even if he had been taken on as a prospective partner by a close friend. I wasn't prepared for this kind of politics, and I was stunned with the realization that it could be an eternity before I would touch any hearts because I didn't have my own cardiologist referral base. My new mentor wanted me to develop my own referral base, for which I had no skills or help from him.

I determined that it would be years before I had much of a practice with this man. I was already thirty-five years old, and most surgeons have only twenty years of productive surgical practice. So there I was, champing at the bit to perform surgeries and care for patients, while my new senior partner protected his patient base like a hen watching her brood. In my first three months, I probably handled two or three small cases. The only way I was using up my energy was jogging eight to ten miles a day, sweating out my frustrations instead of taking them out on my friends and family. I was a very unhappy man. I got along with my new employer, but I suspected we viewed life in fundamentally different ways, and he confirmed my suspicion the day he told me that his main goal in life was to be worth $4 million by the time he was fifty. Then he would just hang it all up. That's what he wanted out of life. What I wanted then, and still want today, was to care for patients. I knew our goals weren't compatible. Still, I didn't tell him. I was afraid to. And I didn't tell Kay because I thought she wanted to stay in her new home. That led to more frustration. I wasn't prepared for this kind of politics. I couldn't hide my unhappiness. The surgeon found out how I felt through mutual colleagues, and Kay soon sensed my unhappiness, too.

"You're not happy, are you?" she asked one night at dinner.

"No, I'm not," I replied. "I don't enjoy working here. In fact, I have no work. I don't see any future here. I have all this skill and no patients."

"Well, just leave," she said. "I need a happy husband, not one who walks around here with a long face and slouched shoulders."

"Do you mean that?"

"Yes, I do."

And we did.

Kay later told me that she never thought the partnership would work. She hadn't received "good vibes" during a dinner meeting with the surgeon, she said. Perhaps women are more sensitive than men. Or perhaps I was just too eager to join a surgical practice and get started.

We looked back to Des Moines, where I had been happy in my general surgery training. I knew several general surgeons at Iowa Methodist there, and I knew the hospital was probably in need of a young heart surgeon. There was just one group of heart surgeons in Des Moines at that time, at Mercy Hospital. The surgeons at Methodist gave me a warm welcome. "This town could use a little competition," they said.

I went to my "boss" and gave him the news. "I don't think I fit in here," I told him.

To my surprise, he didn't act distressed and agreed that an end to the relationship probably would be best. It was a puzzle to me why he wanted me there in the first place. He had no plan to promote me or to expand the business. I felt he only wanted to protect his turf. I suppose it's a common problem in medicine and in many other businesses. Few people want to share what they have built up, and established doctors can be very protective. It's a very human trait, I suppose, but very surprising to a young, idealistic surgeon who had done nothing but train in medicine.

I haven't seen that surgeon since. I know he has a very successful practice. He should. He's a good, fast surgeon. Despite the bad experience, my time with him was not wasted. I learned some new surgical techniques and a valuable lesson: When you bring new doctors into your practice, nurture them, bring them along, make them a part of the team. Hopefully, they will become even better than you.

I was excited about my move to Des Moines, excited and full of energy, even though it was our ninth move in a little over ten years. Three general surgeons at Iowa Methodist in Des Moines hired me and promised to help me as much as they could. It was quite a contrast in attitude from my previous experience. They made me an associate, with the idea that I could strike out on my own and form a cardiac surgery group if I found someone else in my specialty. Their attitude affected me, and I've felt an obligation to help other young surgeons along ever since.

They introduced me to the cardiologist who had opened the cardiac catheterization lab at Methodist. He had just completed his residency two years before, was very busy, and strongly believed that Methodist ought to have its own heart surgery program.

My heart surgery patients were few and far between at first, and we had to cart them from Methodist to Mercy because of the health planning political situation. There had been an agreement among the hospitals and an area health planning agency that all heart surgeries would be performed at Mercy and all sick newborn babies would be cared for at Methodist. It seemed absolutely crazy to me, especially since Mercy had breached the arrangement by opening its own neonatal care unit. Why should a private hospital have to enter public politics to expand its services? Why should we have to take sick patients and transport them a couple of miles across town from a teaching hospital with 700 beds to a nonteaching hospital with 400 beds? That's what we had to do, and on two occasions our patients died in transit without making it to the operating room.

That was too much for me. That was not how I wanted to practice heart surgery. I was determined to change that setup, as were the surgeons who hired me. We'd sit around and talk for hours about how it was nonsense. Little did we know that the nonsense was about to become official because a "certificate of need" law had been passed by the legislature and was going to take force the very next year.

Dr. Louis Rodgers, one of the surgeons who had hired me, called me at home one night, about midnight, after reading the new law. He said he felt he needed to talk to me right away.

"Ron," he said, "we need to start heart surgery at Methodist soon or we'll never be able to do it there. As of July 1, 1978, you will need a certificate of need, and you'll have to prove before a board of federal and state planners that you have the numbers and the need for a heart surgery unit."

Lou added that he thought the health planning council would favor Mercy's heart surgery monopoly. We would not be able to establish our own cardiac surgery unit unless we acted quickly and decisively, he said.

We started making plans to perform heart surgery at Methodist, and rumors of our plans started leaking out. Calls started coming in from health planning officials. Meetings were set up. There were powerful forces trying to stop us—the federal government, the state, the county, health planning officials, the president of Blue Cross and Blue Shield, and officials at Mercy. They were all asking questions about what we were planning, and they were all telling us emphatically that we couldn't perform heart surgery at Methodist. They knew they had no law to stop us, not until July 1, and we knew we had to hurry to get our unit started before the new law took effect.

It was a race against time. Mercy officials tried to stall us by saying we should come to some new sort of agreement. Blue Cross and Blue Shield officials backed Mercy. We kept pushing forward, even though Methodist's administrator was very concerned about the public image this fight would create for his hospital. We told him in no uncertain terms, using a few four-letter words, that it was fine to worry about public image, but worries about patient care should come first. It was ridiculous to move critical patients from one hospital to another when there was room, and plenty of patients, to perform heart surgery at both.

No one wanted to believe us when we told them there was a need, but in 1978, when we started at Methodist, Mercy was performing 300 surgeries a year and we performed 125. Today, we're performing well over 500. Competition is keen, and heart patients have benefited, even though our practice at Methodist opened a wide breach between Methodist and Mercy that has persisted through the years.

I teamed up with Dr. Hooshang Soltanzadeh, an American from Iran who had been in this country for twelve years. I felt we complemented each other very well. He was neat, an impeccable dresser, and I was happy in any kind of attire. He was quite conservative, and I was more liberal. He wouldn't take many chances, and I was a bit of a risk-taker. He had more experience in cardiac surgery, and I was just beginning, so I could draw on his experience. He was technically good in some ways and I was technically good in others. We developed a give-and-take relationship that has allowed us to grow and thrive together.

We selected our first surgery patient, explaining to him what we planned to do. He knew the political situation, and he accepted it. In fact, he was thrilled to help make history by being our first patient at Methodist. We recruited a perfusionist, the expert who runs the heart-lung machine, and we agreed to buy the instruments and heart-lung machine needed for the surgery. Methodist provided the support staff. All this was done as secretly as possible. Nobody knew exactly what day we were going to operate, except that it would be before July 1. On that day, the certificate of need law would take effect, and Medicare could withhold money from the hospital unless we were already performing the surgery or had the certificate of need.

D-day was June 19. Our first heart surgery at Iowa Methodist went with Swiss-watch-like precision. Unknown to us, health planners were in town that day from all over the state. They were meeting to discuss our situation, along with other expansion projects. When they found out we were performing surgery on the day they were in town, the meeting became a hornet's nest, filled with the buzz of angry planners. Everyone decried the duplication of services. It hit the newspapers, radio, and TV. Health planners, politicians, and officials at all of the other hospitals criticized our "duplication of service." The angry buzz traveled right into court, where health planners, along with state and federal agencies, tried to block our way with temporary injunctions. But we were within the law. We had begun before July 1. We performed four surgeries that week, and all our patients survived. We did this while public opinion raged against us, the hospital, and the hospital staff. In an effort to stop us, state and federal planners filed lawsuits against us, the chief of medical staff, and the hospital. We felt we were right, so we took the pressure.

Even some doctors carried the attack against us, claiming in newspaper articles that our mortality rate would be high because we had a new program with just a few patients. Their claims couldn't have been farther from the truth. Our first 206 open-heart cases were performed without a fatality, but we were still in court because the health planners would not let the issue die. They had their noses smashed, and they were stinging. They wanted to save face and look good. At least that's the way it appeared to us.

Attorneys' fees were mounting on both sides. Our side spent $8,000 in the first year alone. Solutions were offered by consultants, planners, and hospital administrations. One offer was to combine the programs and make ours a satellite of Mercy's. We wanted nothing to do with that, except maybe as a last resort. Eventually, we agreed to take it through health planning channels and have it reviewed. The agreement stated, however, that we would continue to perform heart surgeries, and would continue to generate the numbers to justify our program. Our heart unit was approved, but not until we went through dozens of meetings and media blitzes in which consumer groups, health planners, government officials, and other hospitals were overwhelmingly against us. But no one could deny that we had performed 206 cases without a fatality. We held that record up and used it as our shield. Even so, if the health planners had had their way, Des Moines would not have two fine heart programs today. In my view, patients in need of top-notch heart care would have been the losers.

In my view and in the view of many others in health care, the health planning bureaucracy gobbles up more and more health care dollars for bureaucratic bungling and jumbling. Dollars that could be used for health care are being used to shuffle paper, and it could get worse as the planners add new layers of bureaucracy to branch out from cost control into quality control.

The politics of government "quality" monitoring, in fact, could produce two striking paradoxes: (1) It could make some of the nation's best heart programs look worse than average ones. (2) It could lead to lower quality care.

Let me explain through a couple of personal experiences. In the first, a group of doctors preserved their "quality" record by choosing not to perform surgery on a high-risk patient. In the second, I made a choice that could have damaged my record and increased the mortality rate for Methodist's heart program. Here are the stories:

I was in my office, trying to dig my way through paperwork that had accumulated during the week. It had been a busy week. I hadn't seen my secretary for three days, and I could tell by the tone of her voice that she was frustrated by the growing paper backlog. Yes, she finally had me behind my desk, plowing through stacks of charts, letters, and papers. Then the phone rang! A welcome interruption to my silent paper drudgery. I grabbed the phone, hoping for an excuse to quit. It was a woman I knew, and she was obviously distressed.

"Dr. Grooters?" she asked. "Can I talk with you for a minute? I hate to bother you, but I have a problem with my mother. I need your help, if possible."

"Yes, go ahead. I'd be glad to help if I can," I reassured her.

She began by describing the condition her mother was in three days before—almost dying of sudden heart failure in another hospital and miraculously being rescued from death. While riding in the car with her daughter, she had suddenly become short of breath and had begun to sweat and turn blue. They were only blocks from the nearest hospital, to which the daughter drove at a high rate of speed. She knew her mother, a charming and until then a vigorous seventy-year-old woman, was starting to die. She screeched to a halt at the emergency room entrance, jumped from the car, and crashed through the door, screaming for immediate help for her dying mother. Attendants and nurses rushed to the car, opened the front passenger door, and found the elderly woman slumped over, blue and dripping with cold sweat. Quickly, the attendants grabbed her and lifted her onto a cart, clamped an oxygen mask over her face, and pushed frantically through the doors and down the emergency room hallway into a treatment room.

"I was certain my mother would die!" the daughter exclaimed. "But she started to recover almost as suddenly as she was stricken."

The woman's mother was admitted to the hospital, and her family doctor finally arrived to take over her care. He shook his head. How did this happen? A puzzle. One moment near death, the next just fine.

"It must have been your heart acting up," he told her. "I feel you need to see a cardiologist while you are here. No delay."

That evening, the heart specialist came. He told the woman's mother that she must have a very bad heart, but he couldn't be sure without performing a cardiac catheterization. He scheduled one for the next day, and all went smoothly. The woman went back to her room after the test, and she and her daughter sat, staring at each other with apprehension as they waited for the results. Both were expecting the worst but hoping for good news. Both were willing to take a risk, if necessary, to prevent another deathlike event like the one in the car.

The cardiologist and the family doctor entered the room together with serious looks on their faces. They stood at the foot of the woman's bed, looking down at her, as if trying to get up the nerve to spell out the bad news.

"I am sorry. I don't think we can help you. Your heart muscle is very bad and your blood vessels are severely blocked. Both are so bad, it would be too risky to perform surgery or the balloon procedure," the cardiologist told her.

Her family doctor nodded in agreement. "I think you might just as well go home and enjoy your last few months with your family."

The jolt hit hard and fast. The woman and her mother were stunned. No help available? How could this be? She had survived, just to be told that nothing could be done, that her days were numbered?

That night was sad, but the woman's daughter also was smoldering and considering a second opinion. She called the family doctor at home and told him she wanted a surgeon to look at the results of her mother's "cath" test. He agreed, and a cardiac surgeon in that hospital was called the next day. His opinion was the same. He confirmed what the others had found: Nothing would help.

So here was this woman, on the phone with me, unwilling to give up on her mother so easily. I could almost see and feel the tears in her eyes and on her cheeks as she told the story.

"Can you help? Can you look at my mom's tests? Please?" she asked.

I couldn't say no. My heart melted, but I knew I couldn't let my emotions sway my judgment. I couldn't give her a positive answer if there really wasn't anything I could do. The situation sounded bad to me, too, but I agreed to take a look and asked her to arrange to have the catheterization films sent to my office, the next day, if possible.

I drove home that night, wondering if I might be of help and also fearing that I might get in the middle of a controversy. Once home, I thought no more of it. I was with my family, enjoying my time with Kay, Dawn, Julie, and Lori.

The next morning, I was performing surgery. Everything went fine. I made my rounds, more tests to look at, more surgery. My mind was occupied with continuous work and my patients of the day. I hadn't given the woman and her mother a moment's thought until my pager went off and I was called to my office.

"The films and medical reports are here to look at from the other hospital," my secretary reminded me, "and the woman's daughter has already called to make sure they're here. She sounded very anxious."

Well, I'd better get this over with, I thought to myself.

At the office, I grabbed the films and returned to the catheterization laboratory, where the viewing machine was. Within ten minutes, I was shaking my head in disbelief. This woman was not that hopeless, not that high a risk. Bad, yes, but with a good chance of being helped. That was my opinion.

I picked up the phone and paged one of the cardiologists I routinely work with. Soon, he was down in the lab, reviewing the films. I didn't say a word. I wanted his opinion without any input from me.

"This woman is operable," he said.

"That's what I thought, too!" I exclaimed. "But this woman wasn't given any hope."

The cardiologist couldn't believe it. We decided to have the films reviewed by another cardiologist, and by one of my partners, another cardiac surgeon. Everyone came to the same conclusion: Surgery could help this woman. It would be a high-risk operation with maybe a 5 or 10 percent fatality risk, but success could give this woman several more years of healthy living.

I called the daughter and gave her our assessment. She was ecstatic, almost uncontrollable, crying with happiness. I tried to bring her back down to earth, explaining that her mother had a good chance, but she could die in surgery.

The surgery was scheduled for the next day, and her mother was transferred to Methodist that night. I saw her, explained the procedure and the risks involved, and went home. At 5:00 A.M. my alarm jolted me awake. I could hardly wait to get to the hospital to see if we could fix her. The operation was successful, and one year later the woman was still healthy, going for walks, driving her car, and taking care of herself.

Did the other hospital's team really believe she was not operable, or did they not want to take on a high-risk case that could damage their success rate? I can't answer that, but I can say such considerations will weigh more heavily, perhaps affecting life and death decisions and leading to a denial of care for those who need it most, as health planners escalate their "quality" monitoring.

I know, too, that the following case could be viewed as a black mark on my record because I chose a chance at life instead of certain death. I decided to act when I could have done nothing, with no argument from anyone. Here is the story:

We sat, with a sigh of relief, patting ourselves on the back after a long, hard day in the operating room. The perfusionist and I had just finished a difficult

96

emergency bypass operation, successfully saving an elderly woman. It felt good to relax and put my feet up while catching my emotional breath and venting stress.

"Whew! Am I glad that one's done."

The perfusionist nodded in agreement. Then my pager went off: the O.R. room phone rang simultaneously. "You're wanted in the cath lab! Now!"

"Now what!" My heart sank and my tired mind rebelled. "Isn't this over?" I could hardly move. I'd been going since 5:30 A.M. Now it was 6:00 P.M. "Do I have to start all over? I hope not." Almost simultaneously a burst of energy hit me! From the sound of the nurse's voice on the phone, it was obvious that someone was in deep trouble in the cath lab. I made a hundred-yard dash, blood rising, heart pounding, wondering, *What's this doing to me, my arteries, my blood pressure?*

No time to worry about that now. My fears were realized in the worst way. The cath lab nursing crew scurried frantically! For here was a patient with no heartbeat rhythm, no blood pressure, unconscious, blue, gulping air in the last agonal gasps of death.

As I entered, one of the nurses, a big man with beefy arms, jumped on the table and started pumping on the man's blue chest. Another was trying to clamp a mask on his face in an effort to force oxygen into his lungs. She was having very little success. The chest compressions were forcing air out of the lungs. The man was stiff as a board, biting down on his tongue, and regurgitating green bile between his teeth and through his nose, natural reflexes for a dying man.

What a way to meet a patient! I thought. *It would have been nice to know this was coming!* But no time for criticizing, only time to help a patient and another doctor. I shouted for the endotracheal equipment so I could insert a tube into the man's airway, making it easier for him to breathe. It wasn't easy. The man's windpipe would expand and contract with each resuscitating compression by the nurse. His tongue would flap in the way. Saliva and green bile would obscure his windpipe. It seemed like a long time, yet it was just a few seconds before the tube was inserted.

As I was attempting the intubation, the cardiologist shouted pertinent information. He had dilated the man's arteries three months earlier. At that time, he hadn't thought the man was a good surgical risk. Now, because he was still having chest pains, he was here for a repeat treatment. Through all the commotion, the cardiologist described what he'd done. He'd successfully dilated the most important artery and was trying to dilate another blocked artery when suddenly the patient began to experience chest pain. He took another picture of the coronary arteries and found that the previously opened artery was blocked. Just about then, the patient arrested. The cardiologist was shocked! A regular heartbeat returned momentarily, but as the cardiologist tried to open the first artery, the patient arrested again and didn't respond to electroshock.

"That's when we called you!" he exclaimed. With his voice shaking a little, he tried to maintain his composure.

This would be a forced job. "How old is he?" I yelled.

"Sixty-eight."

"In otherwise good health?"

"Some chronic lung disease."

"You think he's still viable?"

We looked at the monitor. All we saw was the pulse

reflecting the compressions by the nurse riding the man's chest.

"I mean, was he a functional man before this happened?"

"Yes."

"Well, do you want me to try to save him?"

I felt saving the man was still a possibility, although remote, at best fifty-fifty.

"Well, I—" he hesitated. "I think you'd better. Can you give it a try?"

"Good! Call the O.R. now! We're coming!"

Someone rolled a cart in. We slid the man onto the cart. The nurse, the 200-pound man, jumped on board, straddling the man's chest, and started pumping on his chest as we moved, dragging tangled intravenous lines, EKG wires, and oxygen tubing. The nurse kept pumping. He hadn't tired yet. Only three to five minutes had passed since my pager exploded. It already seemed like hours.

Away we went! Out the doors, navigating the cart with IV poles on wheeled tripods dragging behind. Like navigating a big ship in a small harbor. We tried to move fast, but the IV pole, oxygen tank, all the tubing, and one of the four nurses couldn't make it around a corner. We'd lurch ahead, and then someone would yell, "Hold on! Hold on! Wait for the IV!" We'd stop, get coordinated again, and then head down the hallway as fast as we could go. The cardiologist, meanwhile, left to talk to the unfortunate man's family. I knew they had no idea what was happening.

He had the hardest task. I'd been there before, and *this case might put me there again*, I thought. I kept telling myself, *Hey, we've saved patients like this before! Don't quit now!*

Into the O.R. we went. Very little was ready. It usually takes thirty minutes to get an operating room ready for elective coronary surgery. We had to do it in four or five if this man was to have any chance at all. Everyone was frantically trying to prepare the room when we hit the door, and this seemed to destroy any coordination the operating room nurses had. "Keep it simple, and keep it relaxed" was my thinking. All I wanted was to have this man transferred to the operating table, painted with antiseptic, and draped with two sheets while a knife was placed in my hand. I shouted the orders loudly, but calmly and with authority, taking care not to shatter the nervous confidence in the room.

The main goal was to get this man on the heart-lung machine, which would give his heart a chance to recover. I needed to get him there within the next five minutes. No easy task. It was cut and go.

The steps. Move the body. Keep pumping on the chest. Paint the patient. Keep pumping. Drape rapidly. Keep pumping. "Knife!" Cut the sternum. Keep pumping. Don't worry about bleeding. "Sternal saw!" Pull it through. "Retractor!" Great! "Knife!" Open the pericardium, the sac around the heart. Quick! Get my left hand on the heart! Keep squeezing the heart. Left hand getting tired, making me realize how much work the heart muscle does, and does for decades, before wearing out. Sutures needed to get the pericardium out of the way. Quick! Two sutures to hold the cannula in the aorta and the right atrium. Keep pumping. When will we get through? "Heparin, please!" "Knife!" Now a cannula for the aorta. Keep pumping the heart simultaneously. Don't want to lose the brain. Heart not moving. Looks bad. Quick! "Atrial clamps!" "Go on, pump!" Wow! This is a tough way to make a living! We're

100

now on pump. "Okay, everyone relax." Let the heart recover. Now, let's put a twenty-gauge cannula in the obstructed artery, give that part of the heart a drink, if possible. Heart not beating yet. Ten minutes gone by. This part of the heart needs blood now! Not moving. Really stunned.

Slowly, the heart starts to recover and feebly regains contractibility. Now I could relax for a bit. I knew we'd have to support the heart for a considerable amount of time before we insulted it again with bypass surgery. Now I could clean up, step out of the O.R. and take a look at this man's angiograms, the pictures of his heart taken by the cardiologist. Yuck! The vessels look bad. The cardiologist was right—not an ideal surgical candidate. Only a salvage operation would be possible. Not everything can be bypassed this time. I knew this heart couldn't take the insult that a stable heart would take. We needed to keep the time used to place bypasses on the coronaries as short as possible. While the heart was recovering on the heart lung machine, I sat outside the O.R. relaxing and drinking a Coke. I knew we still had a long way to go. I kept glancing at the man's EKG. Slowly, the heart recovered from no rhythm at all to an occasional beat. Twenty minutes. Thirty minutes. Then suddenly the beat picked up. This heart was finally recovering, with lots of help from us and the heart-lung machine. For a full hour, the heart was supported. Now it was looking very strong: heart rate of eighty to ninety per minute and good contractions.

Now, the repair could begin. Slowly, we cooled the patient's heart by cooling his blood going through the heart-lung machine. Next we clamped the aorta and introduced a very cold solution of glucose and potassium into the coronary arteries. The heart slowed as its temperature dropped to a level that would hopefully prevent further damage and preserve the muscle while we performed the bypass surgery. We pumped 4 degrees centigrade solution through the coronary arteries to cool the heart even more. Down the temperature went, 30 degrees, 25, 20, 15, 10. Cold enough. Three arteries were targeted for bypass, the completely obstructed one first, then two others. It took longer than I liked. The vessels were awful, very diseased, with hard yellow plaque, making it difficult to make a good bypass. I felt my tension increasing, but I had to remain calm. Great acting. Even fooling myself. Some emotion broke through as a suture twisted and knotted. "Damn!" I knew this man's only chance was on the line, and little things were holding me up, keeping me from getting the vital bypasses in place so the heart could be fed its vital blood supply. At least thirty-eight minutes passed. I could release the clamp on the aorta, allowing blood back to the vessels supplying the heart. The three grafts were completed. Now, warm the heart and start the recovery. Hell! the heart is stunned, not beating! Hope! Hope! Time. More hope! Sweat! Cramps in my legs. Take a break. Go to the john. Let the heart recover with help from the heart-lung machine. Trust it.

This has been a long week. Now Friday, 9:00 P.M. Started this three hours ago. Don't poop out now! Recover! Slowly, the heart makes its way back, but the acid test is yet to come. Beating is not enough. It has to take the work load. Sixty minutes go by. Is it enough time? Will it do the work? No guts, no glory. Let's try it. We can't be on the pump all night.

Slowly, the weaning process begins. Five liters,

four liters, three liters. The artificial heart-lung machine begins transferring the work load back to the sick heart. Soon it fails. Strained. Dilated. No go. Go back on pump! The heart empties. Contractibility returns. The heart looks relieved, knowing it doesn't have to work so soon.

Another ten minutes go by. Okay! Start the Adrenalin. The heart begins to beat faster and harder. Okay, fill the heart! Off pump! A minute later, the heart slows, pressure drops, and the heart dilates and fails. Back on pump! Okay, call for the intra-aortic balloon pump. This device, inserted in the man's aorta, will counterpulsate, taking about 25 percent of the work load, giving the heart a chance to recover. Twenty minutes later, it's functioning well.

Okay, let's try again. Five liters, four liters, three liters, two liters. Blood pressure, 80 systolic. Good! Hold at two liters awhile. Heart rate 90, blood pressure 85 systolic. Heart not too full. Okay, come down slowly to 1.5 liters. Okay, 1 liter. Hold! Watching the heart. Hang in there! Blood pressure, 86 systolic. Okay, easy now. Come off bypass slowly. Eight-tenths of a liter, five-tenths. Okay, off!

The perfusionist exclaims relief. Now, watching the heart, I know from experience that things are not over yet. The heart looks a little full. It's still struggling. I notice the front of the heart is straining, not contracting well. We'll need some luck. Blood pressure, 82 systolic, heart rate 90. Okay protamine ready! We need to reverse the blood thinner or the patient will bleed to death. Slowly, slowly, don't reverse it too fast. The heart strains. Blood pressure 70 systolic. Okay, add more dobutamine (another Adrenalin-like substance). Good!

After a few minutes, the sick muscle looks better. Blood pressure is back up to 85.

How's the hemoglobin? The potassium? The blood gases? The pulse "ox" symmetry? Is he still very acidotic? Base deficit or excess? These are all vital indicators that can change quickly. We need to be ahead. Don't want to play catch-up here. No overtime period here, only life or death at the end of this game. The cardiologist can't believe we've brought him this far. "Nice job!"

"Lucky," I say. "Damn lucky!" *Damn stressful, too*, I say to myself. Sometimes I wish I were back in my little hometown, working in my dad's blacksmith shop.

The patient hangs on through the night and through the next day. I'm hopeful, but then it becomes apparent that he isn't going to wake up. Pupils dilate, then become fixed. No reflexes. No hope. The brain is gone.

He starts to deteriorate. Blood pressure down. Down. Down to nothing. He's gone. Dead. All that work. All that hope. All that heroic effort by so many. All that technology, time, and expense. Yet he's gone. Another failure. Death. Silence. A sobbing family. Hugs. Love. Empathy and tears.

Episodes like this are not that uncommon today—not for me, not for any heart surgeon at a hospital with a busy heart program. In fact, the best surgeons at the best hospitals may have the highest mortality rates. We're getting better but losing more patients. It is the most striking of many paradoxes in our profession.

Consider: In coronary bypass surgery's early years, from 1968 through 1974, the mortality risk for patients was very high, over 20 percent. With the advent of advances like cardioplegia (a way of cooling and

Finally, after what seemed like an eternity, the operating room was ready, and one of my general surgery associates helped with the harvesting of veins from the leg for use in the bypass work. Dr. Hooshang Soltanzadeh, another heart surgeon who would eventually become my partner, assisted.

The surgery went well but progressed slowly. The time needed to perform the five grafts seemed to take forever. With every stitch, my arms felt heavier and my nerves got tighter. It was not only a high-risk case, but to make matters worse, the man was the father-in-law of a close friend of mine, a member of our medical family, so I felt even more pressure than usual.

I'm normally cool and confident in surgery, but I felt like I was sweating gallons of blood as I slowly proceeded this time. The surgery was sucking the life out of me. The pressure was weighing me down, making me feel more like a plodding hippopotamus than an energetic surgeon as the clock struck midnight.

We finally finished, and I released the clamp to the aorta, allowing blood to return to the heart, to give the heart a drink. To my dismay, an ugly pattern of heart damage appeared on the oscilloscope screen, and it didn't improve with time, as it so often does. It just stayed there, flashing the same message time after time: injury, injury, injury. When the patient was warm, we tried to wean him from the heart-lung machine. Again, the warning sign on the screen: Injury! Injury! Injury! Back on the heart-lung machine again. I was numb, in a cold, clammy sweat, with an unpleasant tingling feeling rippling through my body.

Hooshang offered encouragement, but I was not comforted. Questions raced through my mind: What would I tell the family? How could I explain? Was it my fault? Should I have given this man to someone with a little more experience? I kept on answering, "Yes." This was too soon. And I kept on answering, "No." It would have been a difficult case for anyone. It was my time, even though I had performed just a few dozen routine surgeries so far.

I stepped back and took a deep breath. After twenty or thirty minutes, we tried to wean him from the bypass machine again with an Adrenalin drip, hoping this would be the tonic the heart needed. I also had put in an intra-aortic balloon pump to help take the work load off the heart. This seemed to help. The man was weaned from the heart-lung machine, just barely, with his heart struggling to pick up the work load and maintain his blood pressure. His EKG looked ugly, however. It was hard to believe he had any blood pressure at all. I started to close. I was starting to feel like a hero, although deep down inside I knew I wasn't. I knew this man's heart had been damaged, either before we put him on the operating table or during surgery. Finally, after five hours of surgery, I went out to talk to the family. I told them he had made it, so far, and saw deep sighs of relief as each one absorbed the news.

The man continued to hang on. After about six hours, though, we had to increase his medication. It seemed to help. He stabilized for a day or two. The signs looked good, so good that I decided to remove the intra-aortic pump. In retrospect, that may have been a poor call. I may have removed it too soon. His blood pressure slowly dropped, and we had to increase his medication. After another twelve hours, he really looked sick. He was gray, and he was picking at the sheets. He required more medication. I swallowed my pride and told the family we needed to put the balloon pump back in. I did it, but by then it was too late. His heart was giving out and couldn't maintain the load.

The night before his death, the nurses on duty called me at home, time after time. "What do we do now?" "What about this?" It was overwhelming. I lay wide-awake, waiting for the phone to ring again, racking my brain, wondering what to do next. I would doze off and wake up to a cold sweat, trembling, almost out of control. I kept wondering. Would this be my first death in Des Moines? Could someone else have cared for this patient better than I had? I almost wished I could trade places with the man. But there was no detour around the situation. I would just have to wait, hope, and pray. Finally, I jumped out of bed and went into the hospital, hoping I could help the man and his family. I couldn't do either. There was nothing I could do. I wanted it to be over with. I wanted him to die or recover quickly. It was too much agony for me. "Get it over with, damn you!" I couldn't stand this pressure night after night. There was no one else to take the calls. Just me.

Gradually, he slipped away. The end came. He arrested and died. Relief for both of us, but the disappointment, despair, and self-doubt and self-criticism persisted for weeks—more sleepless nights, more lying awake asking myself over and over what I could have done differently.

Fortunately, at least for my career and well-being, it seems I have been touched by more miracles than tragic deaths. We doctors probably use the term *miracle* too casually, but every now and then, it seems that a force beyond the surgeon's hands does take over. A miracle does occur. A dormant brain starts functioning. A patient lives who should have died. These miracles, when they occur, replace the exhaustion and desperation with energy and elation. They compensate, in part, for the patients you lose. I would like to share with you a few of the miracles I have been blessed to be a part of:

She was sixty years old, a woman with three strikes against her before we started. She'd had a heart valve replaced eight years before we saw her. Strike one. Somehow, a highly resistant bacterium called *Pseudomonas* had found its way to the valve and had infected it. Strike two. Finally, a large amount of tissue had grown over the valve. Strike three.

The tissue growth had grown over the surface of the valve and had nearly shut it off. There was no question that she needed valve surgery. Her coronary arteries had narrowed, too, so she needed a bypass or two. It would be a tough operation, and I told her so. I explained as gently as I could that she probably had no better than a 50 percent chance of making it through surgery, especially since she was debilitated, with very wet lungs, in addition to suffering from an infection and obstruction around the heart valve.

I had to open the left atrium, or chamber, of her heart to get to the mitral valve. Once opened, however, the valve was nowhere to be found. It was lost under an ugly mass of clot and flesh. I had a sinking feeling, wondering if I could handle this. *Look at that mess!* I thought. *How could she live with this?*

I finally found the old valve. We cut out the artificial valve and the sewing ring, cleaning away excess tissue as we proceeded. Some of the flesh was so rotten and infected, the valve would just come loose without cutting. I'd never seen anything like it and wondered again if I could handle it.

We continued to pick away at all of the loose tissue, hoping there would be some good tissue left. Finally, it was clean, and there was still some tissue to work with, but it was soft. I wondered if it would hold. Each suture was inserted through swollen, soft tissue—through what I couldn't tell—but it seemed to hold. At least a little bit. Now the sutures went through the sewing ring of the new valve. We lowered it into place and tied it down. It was a long, tedious process, one which took twice as long as it normally would because of the condition of the tissue. It seemed to take forever. Finally, the valve was in place, and we quickly moved on to the two bypasses this woman needed. They were routine, a piece of cake. Still, they consumed more time, and I began to wonder if her heart would even start again.

Once finished, we closed and used the heart-lung machine to warm her body. We added some Adrenalin solution to the bloodstream, and her heart picked up. So far so good. We removed her from the bypass machine without much difficulty. It seemed we had pulled her through. We removed the small tubes, or cannulas, from her right atrium. Next, we prepared to use protamine, a substance made from salmon sperm, to neutralize the heparin, the anticoagulant used to prevent clotting while a patient is on the heart-lung machine. Without the protamine, we couldn't even do this kind of surgery. We gave her the protamine and started to see clots immediately. The bleeding slowed, but then it started to pick up. The clots seemed to dissolve as quickly as they formed. Every square inch of the woman's tissue seemed to ooze like a sieve. Every little needle hole started spurting blood. Every raw surface began to ooze. Damn! The clots just seemed to disintegrate. Even cauterization wouldn't stop the bleeding. I wondered: Had her infection caused this? Had the new valve caused this? Had the long surgery caused this? Or maybe a combination of all of those factors?

"Blood! We need blood! We've got a major blood-clotting problem!"

We ordered up lots of blood products, including platelets, the particles in the blood that promote clotting. We ordered frozen plasma, a serum with a high concentration of blood-clotting proteins. And lots of blood.

An hour went by. We'd given her six or seven units of blood, along with fresh plasma and platelets. Still no clotting. Still massive bleeding from everywhere in the chest cavity. My back was sore. My legs were weak. My forehead was sweating, and my ears felt fiery hot. My brain was numb. Why couldn't we get her to clot? We assumed the infection was causing some kind of a breakdown in the clots as they formed. So we gave her more blood. And watched her bleed.

Finally, we packed her whole heart in sponges and went out to talk to the family. I told them we were having a bleeding problem, and we were still trying to stop it. They were grateful for the update, for the news that we were trying everything we could think of to stop the bleeding. I knew there was no way to explain to them what was really going on. They thought that since she was off the heart-lung machine, everything would be fine and the bleeding would be controlled. The last thing they needed right then was a graphic description of massive bleeding.

I went back to the operating room and removed the sponges. She continued to bleed. As fast as we were pouring blood into her system, we were sucking it out of her chest. Damn! It pissed me off! There didn't seem to be anything we could do. My despair grew worse. It all seemed so hopeless. After thirty units of blood, twelve units of plasma, and thirty platelet packs—enough to transfuse the whole city of Des Moines for a day—she was still bleeding.

I sat down in the perfusion room, a small room next to the operating room. I sat with my hands folded. There was nothing else we could do. She continued to bleed. As she was bleeding, the anesthesiologist was pouring in more blood.

I went out to talk to the family again—her daughter and some friends. I told her that her mother was going to die.

"We can't stop the bleeding, and we can't give her more blood because the blood bank is starting to run out."

She was very kind and understanding. Despite her despair, she almost consoled me as I tried to console her. I held her hand for a brief moment and told her we would continue with the same treatment. It was all we could do. Hope was the only thing left.

I went back to the operating room, and her mother was still bleeding massively. The anesthesiologist was giving her the last unit of blood available in her blood type. I sat down again.

"Damn! All that work."

I was mentally and physically exhausted after seven hours of operating and working to keep this woman alive. To no avail. I collapsed into a chair, my mind and body numb. I put my hands behind my neck to get the knots out. I didn't like losing. I hated it. But I had to accept this. She wasn't the first. And she wouldn't be the last.

I sat hunched over, with my head down, resting on my hands. I said a little prayer, just a few informal words for this woman, her daughter, her friends, and for me.

As I sat in despair, the anesthesiologist started yelling out blood pressures. It had been 90. Now it was down to 80. Then 70. It was just a matter of time. Damn! It went down to 60. Then 50. I knew I would be pronouncing her dead any minute. It went to 40.

I might as well get prepared for this one, I thought.

She clung to life with her blood pressure at 40. Then, as if some spirit had entered her body, the bleeding stopped and her blood pressure started to rise. The anesthesiologist was yelling again: "Hey! her pressure is back up to 50! I think her bleeding is stopping!"

I thought, *Oh, come on! don't give me that!*

But it was true. I poked my head around the corner from the perfusion room and saw for myself. Her pressure rose to 55, then 60, then back up to 70. I walked back into the operating room, at first only half believing what my brain was receiving. But then it hit me—the realization of life—and a tremendous surge of energy flowed through my legs, my arms, my entire body. Suddenly, I was gaining a tremendous amount of strength, excitement, and enthusiasm. Elation! Her blood pressure was at 75, and I could remove the packs. I closed her and went back to the family. It had been eight long hours, but this indeed had been a miracle that could not be explained. This woman

116

should have died. Her recovery was beyond my understanding, but it was beautiful.

Another "miracle" involved a slender, healthy, very active woman, just fifty years old, who had a blockage severely restricting flow through her left main coronary artery. Her healthy appearance belied her condition and the history of heart problems in her family. We're talking about a blockage here of the artery that supplies most of the heart muscle, a blockage that could be lethal if not bypassed. The woman had been suffering wave after wave of chest pain at home and had been rushed to the emergency room, where she suffered more pain and was rushed to the catheterization laboratory. My first encounter with her, after being urgently paged, was seeing her writhing in pain on the cath table. The cardiologist had just performed the angiogram, which revealed the severe blockage of the coronary artery. She needed surgery, and she needed it right away. She was too sick and in too much pain to talk, so we went to the family and tried to explain the situation. It wasn't easy. Here was their young, healthy-looking mother who would die without major surgery. Despite their disbelief and the depth of their shock, they reluctantly agreed to let us rush her to the operating room.

The surgery went very well. She was placed on the heart-lung machine without difficulty. Two coronary arteries were bypassed. It was quick, easy, and routine. She came off the heart-lung machine without difficulty. A piece of cake. We brought her back up to the coronary care unit. I wrote my orders and called the other physicians caring for her to let them know she was doing fine. I was proud of myself, and I felt relieved that it had gone so well. I stayed in the coronary care unit

117

another forty-five minutes, just to make sure she was stable. Confident she was, I left. No bleeding. Stable blood pressure. All was well as I departed. She'd even started waking up.

Then, just fifteen minutes later, I received an urgent page: "She's arrested!" I was stunned. "This can't be! She was doing so well." I dashed to the coronary care unit, where I found the resident doctor giving her CPR and several nurses assisting. I took over, and we worked on her for another twenty minutes, pushing her chest to keep her brain supplied with oxygen and jolting her with shock after shock—eight or nine of them—in an effort to restart her heart. Each shock made her body jerk with spasms, as if we were pumping life into her. Yet each time we failed, and each time we wondered how many more shocks she could take without breaking every bone in her body. With the last shock, excrement spurted from her backside, foul green gastric juices and gas erupted from her mouth— and her heart finally started. It was almost as if the smell of death had been pushed out of her body with one tremendous orgasmic spasm. Not a pleasant sight or smell, but welcomed nonetheless.

But why had her heart stopped? She hadn't been bleeding, and she'd been perfectly fine when her heart decided to quit. *I can explore that puzzle later,* I thought to myself. *Better check her pupils first, to see if there's any sign of brain damage.* What? I was startled to see that her pupils were dilated and fixed, an indication of possible severe brain damage. Each was like a black hole. Vacant. Nothing. No sign of life. Empty. Vacuum. She had *no* reflexes. An eerie, sick feeling engulfed me. No hope. Then slender hope. *Maybe this is just a residual effect of anesthesia.* But I knew better. At least two hours had passed since surgery. The anesthesia should have worn off by now. Besides, even if the anesthesia is fairly deep, the pupils aren't usually this dilated.

I had already told the family that the woman had arrested unexpectedly, but that her heart had restarted and everything looked fine. Now, I had other news: the possibility of brain damage. I decided that could wait. I was hoping to go back in an hour or two and find everything okay.

I went back, and she was not all right. Her pupils were large and not reactive to light. They were the eyes of a dead person. Her heart was beating but her brain wasn't functioning. Now I had to talk to the family. I had to tell them what I had found, that it didn't look good. It was a long walk down the hall. The walls seemed to close in on me, and the light green paint grew darker. *God, I hate that color! Why do they paint the walls that awful green?* My legs got heavier. I had to take a deep breath to expand the walls and regain strength in my legs. And to get up my nerve. I had to get my thoughts together. Another sudden change and this one looked permanent. Final.

They were in the waiting lounge. I squatted down to talk to the husband. I told him what I had found. There was nothing else to do. I had to tell him the truth. We would support her heart and other organs until we knew for sure. I told him it looked bad. There was no brain function at all. I stayed around another hour or two. I told the family there had been no change; there was nothing to do but support her and wait a day or two. After a day or two, I said, we might have to turn off the ventilator.

I knew they couldn't comprehend this tragic turn.

It was even difficult for me. There was no answer to the question, "Why?" I sensed they had to be questioning my ability, or at least wondering what really happened during and after the surgery. Their doubts would be natural, but that was little consolation. God! How I wished I could just escape! I felt paranoid as I drove home and had no memory of driving through the city and down the freeway before pulling into our driveway and hitting the transmitter to open the garage door. I sat in the garage a few minutes, trying to take deep breaths, trying to relax, wishing I was in a different occupation.

Kay persuaded me to go out to eat with her, hoping a good meal in pleasant surroundings would ease my mind and allow me to relax. I didn't order much, and I wasn't much company. A long face was all Kay saw. It was 8:00 P.M. I had finished the surgery at 2:00 P.M., six hours earlier. I was physically and emotionally drained. No more phone calls. Nothing. Ten o'clock news time came. Nothing. I called the unit just before bed. Was there any movement, any change, any sign of life? I had to know. Nothing. I went to bed, knowing it was hopeless. I wanted to pick up the phone and call again to see how she was doing. But I knew she was gone. I was positive. Sleep wouldn't come. It wouldn't take me away. I rolled around, one side, then the other, then my back. The sheets grew heavy, then wet with clammy sweat.

I glanced at the clock. Again. Almost 2:00 A.M. Damn! No sleep, just minutes dragging like hours. Then, mercifully, the phone rang. Any news would be better than this!

"What?" It was one of the best phone calls of my life! "What?"

120

"Yes," the voice said. "She's awake and moving. She can't talk, but we gave her a pad and pencil because she kept motioning that she wanted to write! You know what she wrote? 'I saw God.' "

The words sent a chill of joy and hope down my spine, a comfortable chill as if I had been touched by God. The next morning, I drove to the hospital full of energy and went right to the woman's bed in the coronary care unit. She was still hooked up to an IV, a balloon pump, and various other support systems plugged into her body. But she moved. She nodded her head, and when I reached out to her, she squeezed both my hands with hers. She even tried to smile, which was extremely difficult since she had an endotracheal tube coming out of her mouth. Despite all of the tubes and continued difficulties, she seemed to have a divine sense of serenity. And then a nurse showed me the pad: "I saw God."

Several days later, her tubes were removed and she was moved to the regular heart floor. I asked her if she would describe her experience. She said God's eyes were full of love—caring and gentle. And now, she was no longer afraid of anything, not even dying.

I saw her three or four years later. She was doing very well and told me again that she had no fear of dying. To this day, I can't explain her recovery.

Another miracle patient was seventy years old, a woman with a leaky valve and heart disease who had already suffered a heart attack. A very bad combination. The bad valve leaked blood back into her diseased heart, forcing it to work harder and enlarging and straining the heart to the point where it had no reserve. She was in the late stages of heart disease. The mortality rate in such cases, even at the very best hospitals,

121

is 20 to 30 percent. Heart surgeons cringe when they see this combination of heart problems, and this woman was in bad shape—immobilized by shortness of breath and chest pains.

I'd been in practice for about three years and knew I could take on just about anything with the experience I had. Still, this *was* a tough one. The mitral valve insufficiency and leaking was bad enough alone. The coronary disease just made matters worse. I'd *never* operated on both at the same time before. There was, I'm not ashamed to say, just a little anxiety with this one. In fact, we told the woman in all honesty that she might not make it through the surgery. We told her she had just a 60 percent chance. Scary? Yes, indeed, but she had no chance without the repairs. We knew that, and so did she. She and her family seemed to under-stand and accept her dire situation.

We proceeded with the surgery, performing three coronary bypasses and replacing her mitral valve. Whew! So far so good. Then not so good. Try as we might, she would *not* come off the heart-lung machine. Her heart would not take the work load. We tried Adrenalin drips, along with some potent drugs to en-courage her heart to start. Her heart just wouldn't take over. It wouldn't take the load from the heart-lung machine. We inserted an intra-aortic balloon pump, a device that would take 25 percent of the heart's work load. Even with that, we just inched her off the heart-lung machine. Her heart strained like a weight lifter's muscles at the edge of their limit, sustaining a very low blood pressure and pulse rate of about 60 before failing again. Over and over we tried. Four hours. Then five. Then six and seven.

I had gone out to the family once to tell them she

wasn't doing well—a part of the surgeon's ritual to prepare family members for the inevitable bad news to come. I told them we would try a little longer and we would be back with them in thirty or forty minutes. After thirty minutes of resting her heart, we tried coming off the heart-lung machine for the last time. One more try and that would be it. It was useless to go on. We had to face reality. Her heart rate hovered at 60, despite the drugs that should have kicked it to a higher rate. *Maybe that's enough for her*, I thought, because she had gone into surgery with a rate of just 60. Just as I started to adjust to the idea, she deteriorated. Her pressure fell, and her heart rate slowed to 50, then 40.

I gave up and walked out of the operating room and down the long hall to give the family the bad news: "She is dying. There is nothing I can do."

I was holding the woman's daughter in my arms. Her husband was holding her, too. They were both shaking and yet both faithfully said she would be all right. I couldn't understand why they refused to accept the truth. This was it. But it seemed they just couldn't face the reality. As I left, they said they would keep praying.

I felt little more than despair as I gently released the daughter to return to the operating room. I turned to leave, not wanting to look back and yet not wanting to return to the operating room and more bad news. I was certain there would be no life, no heartbeat. Just a cold, lifeless, blue body would be waiting, and everyone would be waiting for me to make the final statement: "Let's quit." That's how it would be; I just knew it, so I took my time. I took my despair and fatigue slowly down the hall, around the corner, and into the operating room, where the sights and sounds were momentarily incomprehensible. Elation! Rejuvenation! Broad smiles, the chatter of excitement and steady beeps of life from the heart monitor. Amazing! Could I afford to believe my eyes? Her pressure increased to 80, then 85, right before my eyes. The person running the heart-lung machine decided to flip the pacemaker on to 80 or 90 beats per minute. It seemed to help! As a matter of fact, her pressure was coming up so fast, we had to turn down the Adrenalin drips. I'd never seen anything like it. It truly was a miracle, albeit one helped with a great deal of surgical time, drugs, and technology. After five days, we weaned her off the intra-aortic balloon pump. It took two weeks to wean her from the ventilator. To this day, I don't understand her recovery.

The woman had two more good years before she died. To this day, I believe there was more than electrical impulses coursing through that pacemaker wire and helping her heart. There was a power I can't explain. Where it came from, I don't know, but I do know that the family was a family of faith, and they had done a lot of praying that night.

Another miracle case began with a call at 4:00 A.M. I wasn't too happy about it at the time. Awakened from a sound sleep, I was told there was a sixty-two-year-old man at the hospital with a dissected aorta who needed help right now. Out of the clear blue! I like to be involved much earlier. I like to have time to prepare for a case like this, time to get my mind in order. It was a shock to be awakened at four in the morning and told by a cardiologist that I needed to come in and fix this guy, now.

This man's problem was brought on by high blood pressure. Excess pressure in the bloodstream had caused a sudden separation, the main artery coming out of the heart had split into two layers. The layers had come apart, creating a shear down the interior wall and sending wave after wave of excruciating pain through this man's body. Screaming, sobbing, crying, and vomiting, he was suffering the kind of pain even morphine won't relieve. The pain of hell. Only a deep sleep or death would relieve his pain.

We put him to sleep and began a race against death. We were sure the artery was weakened and bulging. If not repaired, it would weaken more, then burst, and that would be it. I opened his chest and found the bulging, bleeding blood vessel. It looked like an angry piece of pulsating bologna ready to burst. We inserted a tube into the artery in the groin, and another tube into the right chamber of the heart. This allowed us to put him on the heart-lung machine. Once he was on the heart-lung machine, the threat of the artery's breaking apart was considerably reduced. That done, we cooled the man to 30 degrees centigrade, and then cooled the heart further by clamping the aorta and injecting cold glucose into the root of the vessel. The icy glucose goes into the coronary arteries and cools the heart to 15 degrees centigrade.

Next, we opened the ascending aorta, expecting to find a tear right at the valve. Nothing. We couldn't find a tear. Disappointment, surprise, and terror surged through my body. The tear was supposed to be there! Where was the damn thing? We couldn't just stop, so we decided to expose the aorta and check the back side. As we went around the corner, we ended up in more trouble. My finger went right through the wall of the aorta. I'd found the tear. My finger was in it, way in the back. So there I was, like the little Dutch boy with his finger in the dike. I tried to put stitches in it, but it wouldn't hold. It only continued to tear. We had a clamp on the aorta near the heart, with my finger stuck into the aorta about six inches away. And there was massive bleeding going on! Now what? The only thing I could think of was to cool the man down to 17 degrees centigrade, to shut off circulation to all of the body, including the brain. We often do this, with consistent success, with little children. It's not done often with adults, but in this case we had no choice and went ahead.

I figured once the man was "cold" and void of blood, I could take my finger out of the hole and examine the aorta. Hopefully, we could put this man back together again. It was a long shot. A very long shot. It took forty-five long minutes to cool the body down with the heart-lung machine and a heat exchanger. During all that time, I just stood there with my finger deep in the aortic tear that I couldn't get to because of all the bleeding. Many thoughts passed through my head as I stood and waited, the main one being, *How did I ever get myself into this fix?* This man had been taken to the cath lab by the cardiologist who performed the angiogram that identified the dissection. I didn't have all of the angiogram views I needed, but there was very little time. The man was already on his way to the operating room. The urgency of the situation forced me to compromise. Perhaps this could have been avoided, I thought, if I had been involved earlier on, if I had seen this man and had helped with the preoperative diagnosis. Too late to worry about that now. I hadn't been involved earlier, and now I was paying the price at four in the morning.

The man was cooled down, and we shut off the heart-lung machine. His body was cold. Dead cold.

There was no bleeding now. We sucked up residual blood in the aorta, and that's when we could see where the tear had started. There! It was right where my finger had gone through, down and around the bend, and very difficult to get to.

We exposed it more and opened it with scissors. We took some stitches and pulled the layers together— slow, gentle, easy, trying to avoid rips and tears in the soft, mushy flesh. We had to take our time, yet we had forty-five minutes or less to complete the surgery. Move too fast, and we risked a tear that would cause the man to bleed to death. Keep the man's systems shut down too long, and his brain would surely die. We had what amounted to a limited window of opportunity for life surrounded by walls of death.

Slowly, we pulled the aorta's layers together with carefully placed stitches. They seemed to hold quite well, but the process took a good thirty minutes be-cause the tear was difficult to reach. We then started the heart-lung machine and started warming the man's cold body. We felt pretty good. At the lower temperature, thirty minutes is a safe period of time to let the brain go without blood. Still, I had some doubts because of all the bleeding. Did we cool him quickly enough? It takes a long time with a man his size, a lot longer than it takes to cool a small child.

With the heart-lung machine back on line and the body warming, we continued with permanent repairs to the aorta. It was extremely delicate, just like the early repair when the man was cold. Both layers were like wet tissue paper. Every stitch was difficult. I wanted to hurry, but I knew I couldn't or the stitches would slice like a cheese cutter. If I pulled too quickly or too tight, I'd have another slice in the aorta. We managed to get a graft in, with lots of bleeding from needle holes. After eight hours of surgery, we finally stopped the bleeding.

The man, believe it or not, was awake within four hours after the surgery. In many cases, heart surgery patients don't wake up for twenty-four hours, especially when they were as cold as this man was for an extended period of time. Seven years after the surgery, the man was alive and doing well—a lucky, lucky miracle after what he'd been through.

Suits and Solutions

I'd just completed routine bypass surgery and was sitting down at my desk to collect my thoughts when the phone rang.

"There's someone to see you at the reception desk, Dr. Grooters."

Now what, another medical products salesman? I wondered, striding to the reception area. My minor irritation quickly turned to a sickening feeling of dread as I eyed a sheriff's deputy waiting for me with papers in his hand. I'd just been through a gut-wrenching lawsuit and settlement of several thousand dollars in a case involving a young man who had been in my care. The settlement hadn't been out of line. I'd made a mistake. I could have done better, although I didn't feel I'd been negligent. The young man had been admitted to our trauma center with broken ribs and bruised lungs. He'd been crushed when he rolled his pickup truck while driving drunk. He shouldn't have survived the accident, but he had, and he was recovering under my care when his condition rapidly deteriorated. He had become "septic," an infectious condition producing shock. In his case, the condition had been caused by an infected internal chest wound that no one spotted. We thought his problem was much less serious—a filling of his lungs with secretions due to inadequate respiration. I performed a bronchoscopy to clean out his lungs, but I failed to detect his septic condition. He arrested a few minutes after the surgery. We saved him, but not before he suffered irreversible brain damage. My case was weak. I'd made a mistake, so we settled.

Guilt feelings nagged at me for months, even after I learned that the man had been one of the biggest drug dealers in his area. My oversight still haunts me. After the settlement, however, I resolved to go on with my life and practice. I'd bitten the bullet, you might say, and was then hit with an artillery shell. Out of the clear blue, without warning on June 12, 1986, I was served with papers notifying me that a man and his children were accusing me of negligence and error during heart surgery on their wife and mother.

I walked back to my desk, going blind, arms heavy, mind numb. Every bad emotion overwhelmed me: shock, anger, sadness, depression, disbelief, cynicism, distrust, hopelessness. I sat, staring straight ahead, wanting to be alone for a few minutes. I knew I could regain my composure and think the suit through logically, given some time. Janet Emerick, my secretary, entered my office, wondering if I would be all right. She had faith in me. She cared. In her own reassuring way, she helped me realize I was still a good doctor and a "damn good" surgeon. I needed that.

I remember thinking, *Where is this coming from?* And then looking at the papers and feeling my shock turn to disbelief. I had gotten along with the family that was suing me. I had gone to great lengths to explain to them what had happened—how I thought arterial plaque had dislodged during surgery and had blocked blood vessels, causing a stroke and severe brain damage. I explained that there are other causes for such strokes—possibly air in the bloodstream or shock—but I had no good explanation for what had happened to her. It was tragic, but it was a risk the family was aware of before we performed the surgery.

As I thought back two years, to the day of the surgery and my talks with the family, my disbelief slowly turned to anger, not so much toward the husband and family but toward the lawyer, the s.o.b., that would do something like this. The phone rang. Dr. Mouw, a general surgeon who had harvested the bypass veins from the woman's leg, had received a petition. He'd had nothing to do with the bypass operation, but because he was in the operating room, he was a target in the case.

My partner, Dr. Soltanzadch, had assisted with the surgery and had talked to the family prior to the surgery. He was served with papers when he arrived at the office about an hour later. It wasn't the first time he'd been sued, either, but he was as shocked as I was by this one.

"Can you believe this?" was his first comment to me.

My cynicism got the best of me, and I replied, "People are capable of anything."

The next hour or so was nonproductive as we slumped in our chairs and stared at the walls, at our desks, at one another. The phone rang twice during this time. Dr. Lemon, the cardiologist, was served the same petition, and our perfusionist, the person who operates the heart-lung machines, was named a defendant, too. Both expressed anger and disbelief. They, too, felt nothing wrong had been done, even though the outcome of the surgery had been unexpectedly tragic.

Stroke and neurologic injury during and after bypass surgery are risks we discuss with patients and family members prior to every surgery. Yet the petition claimed we hadn't said anything about such risks before the operation. It also claimed we had performed the operation incorrectly, and said we had not provided proper care after the surgery. The hospital was blamed, too, and later on the company that made the blood oxygenator attached to the heart-lung machine. We all strained to remember every detail. Had we been wrong? Almost two years had passed since the surgery was performed. Could we have forgotten something? Even after a review of the medical records, doubts would creep in.

I called the insurance company claims representative, and again was surprised and amazed. They seemed so calm, sensible and not surprised by my call, as if such suits are filed every day. Business as usual. They asked me to summarize my recollection of the surgery and said their attorney would contact me and the other defendants in a couple of days. I was told to say nothing to anyone about the case.

The lawsuit triggered vivid images in my mind—of the surgery and the miserable postoperative events. Flashbacks of my caring conversations with the family would hit me at all hours of the day, even during surgery. I remembered talking to my partner about his conversation with the woman and her family. She wanted the surgery. The cardiologist had offered her a balloon dilation procedure as an alternative, but we had all thought the dilation and medical therapy would not benefit her as much as surgery. She needed surgery. Three main arteries and their branches were blocked to varying degrees. One was almost completely blocked off.

I had performed bypass surgery on her husband four years earlier. He had done well. She wanted the same treatment and outcome. Since I had operated on her husband, she requested that I perform her surgery. That was fine with my partner.

The next morning, I saw her in the operating room, bright, alert, and in good spirits. I joked with her while we prepared her for general anesthesia, doing my best to make her feel relaxed and comfortable. The surgery went along without a problem—five bypasses, two hours and forty-five minutes "skin to skin," as we would say. Uneventful, safe, smooth—just the way a pilot likes a flight. The bypasses looked perfect, and the heart pumped vigorously. We weaned her off the heart-lung machine without any problems. I almost broke my arm trying to pat myself on the back as I walked down the long hall to the waiting room. I knew most of the time it was like this, but it still felt good because sometimes the walks are long with very sad endings. This time I felt great. I could hardly wait to see the woman's husband. I knew when I saw him I was going to hug him as I shook his hand. I hadn't seen him in three years, and I was glad the reunion with a good patient was taking place under such happy cir- cumstances. Little did I know that two days later I would be explaining to him that his wife must have had a stroke during surgery, and we weren't sure why.

But that had been two years in the past. My colleagues and I faced a much different problem now. We were anxious to meet with our insurance company's attorney, but it was about two weeks after receiving the petition that we finally found ourselves sitting together with Mike Figenshaw to tell him our story. By the time we finished two hours later, I felt we had given him an intense short course in open-heart bypass surgery. I wondered whether he understood what we did and what the limitations of our specialty were. Would he remember all the details, all the things we felt were important? I thought he would need to understand all the technical details and ramifications of the surgery. Little did I know that very little of the information we provided would be used in our defense. During the meeting, after we vented our frustrations and reiterated our conviction that we had done nothing wrong, Figenshaw gave us our first lesson on defending ourselves.

"This is going to take time," he said. "You need to be patient."

I know we were impatient and, being surgeons, we wanted to correct or cut our way out of the problem right now.

"You're good doctors," he reassured us. "Don't worry. Continue to practice good medicine and surgery, and leave the defense up to me."

He said he would handle the defense and would call for help when he needed it. We had the uneasy feeling that it was his show, and we were only fixtures— fixtures and targets. Nevertheless, after the meeting, I did feel I had a little more understanding of how the defense would be handled. I was reassured by Figenshaw's presence and legal expertise, but down deep I was hoping he would persuade the plaintiffs' attorney that his clients had no chance of winning. No such luck. After dozens of depositions, after answering countless interrogatories, after reviewing many scientific articles, I had a strange fear that this legal conflict was going all the way to court, all the way to trial, the place I never wanted to be.

Shortly after our preliminary meeting with Figenshaw, I was again startled by an inquiry from the Iowa

State Board of Medical Examiners. I still remember the date: September 9, 1986. My first reaction was one of paranoia. But then I realized that they, too, had an important function—to maintain quality medical care by licensed physicians. They were not hunting for heads but for problems that might lead them to believe I was an impaired physician. I hadn't realized it then, but I soon learned that any medical malpractice suit filed in the state automatically is sent to the medical examiners for review.

Again, I had to summarize my story, send them my records, and then wonder and worry what their interpretation of the ugly situation would bring. I was relieved two months later, on November 20, 1986, when I received a letter from the board stating that there was "no finding for disciplinary action. File closed. You are required to report to us every adverse judgment and every settlement." This really didn't help so much. The two words *judgment* and *settlement* were not ones I wanted to contemplate at that point.

I heard nothing about the action for about six months after that. The lull gave me a false sense of relief, a feeling that maybe the suit would be dropped. Yet flashbacks of the woman's brain-damaged condition as she lay in bed in spasms, unconscious, intermittently returned, hitting me like a stun gun, causing me to stop whatever I was doing. Fortunately, the image would quickly fade away, and I could go on. Each time, I mentally reassured myself that we had done everything correctly. We had done nothing wrong.

I was just about over the flashbacks and beginning to feel comfortable when a letter, dated April 15, 1987, arrived from Figenshaw, informing me that the family's lawyers wanted depositions from me, the other doctors named in the suit, the perfusionist, and the three nurses who had been in the operating room. The letter said we needed to arrange a deposition date with the plaintiffs' attorney. News traveled fast through the hospital. Anxiety, mixed with anger and frustration, was at its peak.

My deposition date was set for June 30, and the three weeks of waiting were the longest I have ever experienced. Time moved in painful slow motion, but always in the wrong direction, ever closer to deposition day. I almost wished we were living a hundred years ago, in frontier days, so we could settle this matter quickly with Colt .45s. Just strap on the pistols, shoot it out, and have it over with. I knew our team had done nothing wrong in the surgery, but the thought of making a misstatement, of not appearing to be a confident expert, of drawing a blank on a question, frightened all of us. Pardon a trite expression, but I felt I would be like a fish out of water, or worse yet, like a man without clothes.

My deposition was long and laborious, a combination of mundane and routine questions about my education, training, and experience interspersed with lengthy, meandering probes and a few—very few—intelligent, pertinent questions. The grilling went on. The clock's second hand seemed to move like a minute hand, and the minute hand like an hour hand. I kept thinking: *I know we were right. I know we did nothing wrong. When are you going to quit questioning me?* I wanted to yell it out to everyone in the room. "Why? Why are we doing this? Prolonging the pain for the family, raking us over the coals, all for nothing."

Suddenly, it was over. Complete relief. Reassurances from friendly attorneys: "You did well, Ron, just like the others. This is defensible!" they exclaimed.

"But is it right to put me through this?" I muttered.

Again, I thought it was over; at least it felt like it was over. But then depositions, hundreds of pages, kept arriving at my office from Figenshaw. He wanted Hooshang and me to read and critique each and every one. I was most shocked by the plaintiffs' depositions, although I suppose I shouldn't have been. The "expert cardiologist" for the plaintiffs' side strongly felt that surgery had not been necessary. He would have tried medications, he said, but we felt he totally ignored the progression of her symptoms and the fact that she had partial blockages in multiple vessels.

He doesn't care what he says. He's an expert getting paid to say that, I told myself.

Down deep, I hesitated: Had we been wrong? *No, no way.*

Later, we learned that the "expert" had never performed an angiogram. He was relying on another cardiologist to help with his interpretation of the woman's angiograms. The cardiologist's evaluation was not that different from ours, but he was overlooking one fact: When I performed the surgery, we found the vessels were even worse than the angiograms had indicated. This is not uncommon. Cardiologists and surgeons are aware of this, and base their decisions about surgery on many factors—angiograms, symptoms, past medical records. Surely, I thought, this cardiologist must have seen the medical history. Surely, he must have read my operative report.

The most vocal and damaging expert witness was a man who condemned our perfusion technique, saying we had the heart-lung machine set up in such a way that made it prone to "air embolization." He called it "gaseous embolic phenomena," in simple terms, air bubbles in the bloodstream. He felt we should have used a membrane oxygenator instead of a bubble oxygenator. Both were good, as far as we were concerned. He felt we should have used an arterial line filter. About 50 percent of the surgical teams used them, and 50 percent didn't. He said we let the blood get too thin. But we did this all the time, without a problem, to reduce the need for blood transfusion, an important consideration today with the threat of AIDS.

He went on and on: Our perfusionist must have made a mistake. The bubble oxygenator we used was one of the worst on the market, in his opinion. He speculated that the air alarm on the machine may not have been turned on to warn us of air in the system, and that the blood gas in-line monitor may have been inaccurate. All of these opinions, the speculation and borderline statements, were being used to build a case against us. This "whore," as they are called by defense attorneys, could say what he pleased. He could say anything, anything for a fee of a few thousand dollars. After reading that deposition, I knew we were in for a fight. I wondered how a jury would be able to separate fact from fiction, absolutes from debatable techniques.

The trial was scheduled to begin a few months after some twenty depositions had been taken, in September 1988. It was postponed. The plaintiffs weren't ready. It was rescheduled for June 1989. Again, I was nagged with stressful flashbacks and fears about what might happen in court. I knew the year of waiting would seem much longer than a year. The year of waiting, thinking, worrying, and anticipating would take all of the fun out of practicing surgery, would inhibit any freedom of

138

thought. The entire year, all of my triumphs in the operating room, all of my quiet, pleasant times at home, would be darkened by the pending trial.

I was sure I never wanted this to happen again, that I would have to do something about the stroke problem. But what? A partial answer would come to me later, but I knew a complete prevention of postoperative strokes was about as remote as a single cure for cancer.

As the trial approached, activity increased in frequency and intensity like a Doppler effect. A week before the trial, a meeting of three attorneys for our defense and all of the defendants was arranged in our office. For three hours, every point of debate and claim made against us was discussed and rehearsed, and the worst news: We were told the trial was expected to take over two weeks. The plaintiffs' witnesses would be on the stand for more than a week, after jury selection, which was expected to take a day or two. Finally, we would present our defense and our witnesses.

Two weeks. Disbelief and disappointment engulfed each of us like clouds shrouding a mountain. We knew we would have to sit in the courtroom for the duration of the trial. We had patients to take care of and practices to manage, but that didn't matter. Fortunately, in our cardiac surgery practice, we had another good partner, Dr. Kent Thiemen, and a new associate, Dr. Robert Schneider. They would have to do the work of four surgeons for the two-week period. And they did. They worked hard, sometimes sixteen hours a day. They would see us late in the afternoon after the trial had recessed for the day. They would listen to our daily accounts, our thoughts, our frustrations, our criticisms of the witnesses, our descriptions of the

139

boring, laborious approach on dozens of needless questions. They would listen to us describe what we thought were half-truths, misinterpretations, and misstatements from some twenty plaintiffs' witnesses. We felt beat-up each day, more tired than if we had performed surgery for eighteen hours straight.

By the time the plaintiffs finished their presentation, I wondered if we would be believed. Our best hope was that the jury would feel that they had been too critical of everything. According to the plaintiffs, we had done nothing right, and again I was wondering if that were the case. It was as if we were the patients and they were the surgeons, and we were being cut up by the knife of civil law. Each day, our attorneys would reassure us that things were going well: "No need to worry." "Yeah, tell us another one." We felt like members of a football team, behind 35 to 0 at the half, receiving a pep talk from the coach.

Each day, at noon, we would go back to the attorneys' offices, have a quick lunch, and then listen to them tell stories of other trials, victories, and losses. They would try to relax us with humor, but there was nothing to laugh about as far as we were concerned. We were amazed at their casual attitude and their almost cavalier overconfidence. We weren't that sure. We remained skeptics for the entire two and one-half weeks, even after our side had taken the stand.

"Just appear as humble experts and the truth will come out," was Mike Figenshaw's constant advice to me day after day before my appearance on the stand. Easy for him to say, but I felt my bowels churning ten minutes before my scheduled time on the stand, and I headed for the bathroom. The pressure was building in more ways than one.

The plan was to present my story, to explain what heart surgery was all about. Then we would show a video of heart surgery being performed. The questioning continued through the entire morning. As my testimony progressed, my confidence improved. Yet my palms remained sweaty. Then lunch, a quick debriefing, and an afternoon of cross-examination. The plaintiffs' lawyer kept grilling me, asking many questions in different ways to see if I would deviate from my answers and leave him an opening. But I felt he couldn't break me. Finally, it was over. I had told my story, but it was maddening to have my ability, judgment, and techniques so severely questioned. Even after fifteen years of college, medical school, and surgical training, plus seven more years of practice, including 1,500 bypass operations, I still had to sit on a chair in front of a jury, the plaintiff, the attorney, the judge, and other experts, and be questioned and judged.

As the trial entered its final days, a voice inside me kept saying: "You never want to be here again. Never." I reconstructed what I had said on the stand. I had blamed dislodged plaque in the aorta for the fatal stroke. I knew it was true. It couldn't have been air bubbles. The air detectors had been in perfect working order, and we had performed the surgery 1,500 times without air embolization. It had to be plaque. I knew that was the cause of the woman's strokes, but I had no proof.

The trial ended. The jury went into deliberation. I went back to work. The next day, at 2:00 P.M., while I was sewing a coronary artery, the phone in the operating room rang: "We won!" I was jubilant! A warm surge of energy filled my veins. I wanted to say, "Take that!"

to the plaintiffs' lawyer. But at the same time, I knew we all had lost. Most of all, the woman and her family. I found no pleasure in that.

Later, the inner voice came back: "You don't want to be there (in court) again—not for this kind of problem, not for stroke." My subconscious was trying to tell me something, was challenging me to think, to probe, to reflect: "Prove what you said in court. Prove it to yourself."

That was the start of the research that today, as this book is being written, is proving that the strokes during and after heart bypass surgery are being caused by undetected plaque inside patients' aortas.

During the months following our court victory, finding a way to prove the cause of the strokes had me stumped. I can remember watching television one Sunday morning and, by accident, tuning in to a sermon about problems and how we approach them. What struck me was the speaker's positive attitude about problems. They were not problems but "opportunities, opportunities for success." That is paraphrasing what he said, but his sermon stuck with me. Combining that attitude and my experience in court was enough. I wanted to solve this major problem facing heart surgeons and their patients every day: stroke.

Over the course of the next year, I met with the executive vice president of Iowa Methodist Medical Center, a number of physicians with clout, and the hospital's board of trustees. I told all of them the same thing: "We need to research this problem."

Finally, after an executive council meeting of the board of trustees, I was granted $300,000 to conduct cardiac research to see if I could solve some of the problems. I had explained to them that we had some ideas, some avenues to explore. We had found a young Japanese heart surgeon, Dr. Hiroshi Nishida, who could conduct research in the laboratory and organize the clinical work.

So there it was, the money. The elation hit me as I walked out of the boardroom and down the narrow hall on the way to my office. Then a sobering thought: *Yes, I got the money, but now I must produce. Now the responsibility is mine. Now the long, hard hours on top of my practice will begin.*

In addition to the stroke problem, I planned to study wound infections associated with heart surgery, plus new methods to preserve heart muscle during bypass surgery. I had some ideas in those two areas, but I still had no idea how to solve the stroke problem. Constantly, over and over in my mind, the courtrooms appeared. So did the ugly, disappointing appearance of the woman we had lost, lying rigid, twisted, only partially responsive.

Then, one lucky day something happened to nudge me toward an answer. I was inserting a cannula (a tube) into a patient's aorta. As I took the clamp off of the cannula, blood shot out into a pan. There was the answer: Along with the blood were large particles of yellow fatty plaque. I knew immediately: *This is one of those patients at risk, one who could have a stroke during or after surgery.*

I knew in a flash: *I can't perfuse (pump) blood into this man's aorta from the heart-lung machine with the cannula in this position. The pumping action could dislodge more plaque and cause a stroke.*

Surely, he will have a stroke, I thought.

I decided to use a clean, remote location, the femoral artery, a leg vessel, as a way to pump blood

143

into the patient. I explored the artery. It was good. So I removed the cannula from the aorta and inserted it into the femoral artery. No plaque came out of the cannula this time. The operation went without a hitch, and the patient woke up. The surgery was a success.

I was elated but still puzzled: How could I use the knowledge from this one experience to develop a safe, effective screening procedure for each and every patient? Days and nights went by. Still, I couldn't put it together. Pieces were missing. How do I control the amount of bleeding during the test? How do I prevent the plaque from breaking off and flowing downstream to other organs, risking a stroke or other damage during the test? How do I detect the plaque?

Questions, questions, questions. They kept coming and repeating themselves. I was absorbed. My mind would wander during dinner. I wouldn't hear conversations around me or respond when someone spoke to me.

Then suddenly in the quiet darkness, shortly after going to bed around one in the morning, the answer came. I'd just kissed Kay, wished her good night, and given her my love. I turned over and couldn't get to sleep. Questions, questions. The questions obsessed me. I felt I was close to an answer. Close, but not there. Something inside of me would not let me let go, would not let me quit thinking about it. No matter how hard I tried to get to sleep, no matter how many sheep I counted, the ideas and partial answers kept running through my mind.

Suddenly, I sat straight up. A chill went up my spine. I tightened my fist and slammed it down on my right thigh as I exclaimed under my breath: "That's it! I've got it! Damn! I've got it!"

144

There in the darkness of my bedroom, all of the details, the parts, the techniques, and the tools fell into place. I had the answer. All I had to do was make it a reality. Simple: Just insert a suction cannula into the aorta before insertion of the regular perfusion cannula. Rub the suction cannula in the area where the perfusion cannula spurts blood into the aorta. Draw blood with the suction, running it through a filter, and then check the filter. If plaque is present, don't put the regular perfusion cannula in that area. Place it somewhere else, probably in the leg artery.

Just that simple! An easy procedure that would enable surgeons to avoid the risk of dislodging soft, friable plaque that could go to the brain and cause a stroke. I couldn't get to sleep that night. The vision persisted. I didn't know if it would work. I might fail, but somehow that thought didn't bother me. My anticipation and excitement were too great. I was elated that I had finally formed a concept in my mind and couldn't wait for the challenge of making it work.

I knew I would have to have some kind of trial, an indication that the concept would work, before I would be allowed to try it on patients. I needed to test the concept in our laboratory, and I had an idea. It was complex, but I thought it would work.

I went to the pathologist at Iowa Methodist and asked him to save some of the diseased aortas from cadavers after autopsies. This was more difficult than I imagined. The kind of diseased aorta I needed, one with fragile plaquing, was not that common. Acquiring the tissue I needed took two months.

Next came the animal stage of the experiment. There aren't any animals that develop the kind of aortic plaque I would need for my experiment, so the tissue

145

with plaque from the cadaver was sutured in place in an animal's aorta. Then, we conducted the intra-aortic suction procedure. Filters were placed in the cannula and also downstream in the animal's circulatory system. We needed the second filter inside the animal to see if the procedure would free too much plaque, creating the stroke danger we were trying to avoid. Would too much plaque float free during the procedure? We had to know.

I vividly remember the first test. Dr. Nishida and I were almost afraid to remove the castings around the filters. We held our breaths as the filters were exposed.

Wow! I thought.

"Very interesting, I think," said Dr. Nishida.

There it was: hundreds of particles in the suction filter and none in the downstream filter.

"Well, what did you expect?" I said half kiddingly.

Down deep, I knew it would work. I was 100 percent sure! Then, on the other hand. . . . but there it was! Success! A potential advance in heart surgery techniques! But still a long shot to get everyone to accept it, I thought.

Three times in a row, the experiments on animals were successful. No harmful debris downstream. I now had the ammunition I needed to proceed with testing on patients. Now I could go to the hospital review board to obtain official permission to test my concept on patients. I worked hard on my presentation: the magnitude of the stroke problem, the way strokes occur during heart surgery, my testing on animals. Everything needed to be presented methodically and logically. I needed to emphasize the need for the procedure. I needed to demonstrate its safety. I needed to be clear, confident, and believable. No one had ever tried this procedure before. There were no reports on this in medical literature, anywhere.

The day of my presentation, I was like a child with a new toy, bubbling with enthusiasm, exuding confidence. Everything went well, just as planned: orderly, logical, clear, concise. I sat down, expecting a barrage of questions. Silence. What? Everyone understood? It hadn't occurred to me that everyone in the room already agreed that stroke was a devastating, horrible complication associated with heart surgery, and that promising research in this area was sorely needed.

I walked out of the room, wanting to jump in the air, kick my heels, and let out a yell. I was immediately sobered, however, with the realization that the procedure might involve unknown risks. Also, I asked myself, would it really benefit patients? The odyssey was about to begin. The procedure would have to be used on many patients to obtain statistically valid data.

Consent forms were prepared, with help from hospital lawyer Dennis Drake. The equipment was prepared. Mock practice procedures were repeatedly performed with the operating room nurses and the chief perfusionist, Steve Davis. We were ready.

Would the first patient give his consent? Like a bold life insurance salesman unafraid of rejection, I entered his room. He was seventy-eight years old and needed a triple bypass. Would he understand the procedure? Would he have faith in someone he barely knew? Would he permit something being done to him that had never been done to any patient anywhere in the world?

I sat down, took a deep breath, and proceeded to explain why he needed the bypass surgery. Other options of treatment were available, but not recommended, I said. The man's left main coronary artery was severely obstructed. His risk of a fatal heart attack each year was 25 to 30 percent without the bypass surgery. Medicines would not help, I explained, and a balloon procedure would be too risky because it could break plaque free and block the left main coronary vessel, causing a massive heart attack. The bypass surgery procedure itself had a fatality risk rate of 4 or 5 percent, I said, and other possible complications associated with surgery, including bleeding and stroke, added another 10 percent risk.

Then came my sales pitch: "Stroke is the worst complication, and it happens about seven percent of the time at your age. We have just developed a procedure to test to see if you are at risk of having a stroke."

I explained the procedure, describing the insertion of a tube into the main artery coming right from the heart: "We apply suction as we gently probe the inner lining of the aorta in the area where we usually insert the tubing from the heart-lung machine. This part of the test takes about ten seconds, and then we remove the instrument and check a filter in the suction circuit for loose plaque. If particles are there, you are assumed to be at risk of a potential stroke because we believe plaque loosened by the heart-lung machine's pumping action is the primary cause of stroke associated with heart surgery.

"If the filter contains no debris, we proceed with the usual technique, inserting the heart-lung machine tube into the aorta. If we find debris in the filter, we insert the heart-lung machine tube into the main leg artery.

"I don't know all of the risks because we've just started performing this test."

148

I held my breath. I didn't want to tell him he was the first.

"Now, if you want to consider this procedure, please read this consent form and sign it. A nurse who has been instructed in the procedure will stop by and help explain it to you if you have any other questions."

I expected hesitation; but much to my surprise he immediately agreed.

"I do not want a stroke. I would rather be dead," he said emphatically. "If you think this may benefit me, you go ahead and do this procedure on me."

He looked me straight in the eye.

Hell, I didn't know for sure. Would it benefit him? In theory, I thought it would. That was the answer.

"Yes, I think it may benefit you. In theory." My voice was a little jerky. "But we don't have all the answers yet. We don't know all there is to know about risks versus benefits. That is why we are doing this research. Just read this consent form, and if you want to do this, sign it. I don't want to push you. You make the decision. I will leave now. Just read this. I'll see you in the morning."

Then I walked out of the room, hoping he would give his consent. Two hours later, the project nurse, Cynthia Bik called.

"Hey, guess what? This guy believes in you. He is going to sign the form."

I shook. Goose bumps rose on my arms. Again, I had to produce.

The next morning, the procedure went just as I expected. The man tested positive, badly positive, with a large amount of yellow, irregular particles and tiny crystals of cholesterol in the screening filter.

God! I thought. *Already a positive!*

We altered our cannulation, inserting the heart-lung tube into the leg artery. All through the bypass surgery, I kept asking myself: *Will he wake up? Will he stroke?*

After the surgery, I took the long walk to the visitor's waiting room. I showed the filter to the man's wife so she would halfway understand. Now we both wondered how he would do. We all had something at stake—the man his life, the woman her husband, and me the future of my procedure. The first one had to work, I told myself, and then the next and the next, and on and on.

We waited, all of us. My mind seemed to pace, involuntarily, between fear and confidence. We wanted the man to wake up alive and whole. Six long hours went by. He started to move. Tears began to run down the sides of his face as his drowsy eyelids strained to open.

God, I thought. *He is going to wake up. We did it!* was my premature conclusion.

Over the next hours, more life returned. He began to respond to commands: "Move your fingers." "Wiggle your toes." "Open your eyes." He did everything. He passed the tests. I passed the test. We were on our way.

What energy! What elation! I had to refrain from yelling, "Great!" as I stood in the intensive care unit surrounded by nurses, sick patients, and the man's wife and family. Yes, we were on our way. Now we had to produce. We had to reduce the number of strokes.

In the following fifteen months, we performed the procedure 200 times. In 10 percent of those patients, we found a large amount of plaque in the filter and altered our procedure, placing the heart-lung machine cannula in a leg artery. We've had some strokes, but the rate is down substantially. We've reduced the stroke rate in the seventy-year-old age group from about 7 percent down to 1.5 percent.

Neil Harl: One Patient's Story

I was half an hour late for the appointment and half expected Neil Harl, a well-known university economist, to be gone by the time I arrived at the office. After all, one of my junior partners could easily have taken care of his questions and concerns. But he was still waiting when I arrived. He hadn't wanted anything to do with my young associate. He wanted to see me and no one else. His attitude was flattering. It boosted my ego, but at the same time it made me suspect I might be dealing with a Type A person. I wasn't surprised at all, when I went into the exam room to introduce myself, to find Neil to be a little high-strung and noncommittal, seeming to demand answers with perfection.

As I do with most patients, I let him do the talking initially, and answered as many probing questions as I could. There was no question that he needed bypass surgery, but he wanted to be sure of that. There also was no question that he was in a low-risk category—relatively young at fifty-six with no apparent heart damage—but he wasn't going to take that for granted, either.

He made it clear from the beginning that he was going to seek a second opinion, and I didn't discourage him at all. I didn't believe a second opinion was necessary, but I didn't tell him that. His approach, it seemed to me, was rational and intelligent. He was articulate and had a keen insight into his problem.

I don't recall how the subject came up, but it came out that I had been doing some research into cardiac surgery in addition to my private practice. This seemed to be reassuring to Harl, a scholar who respects the inquiring mind. After I had finished my description of the surgery and the possible complications and risks, we chatted awhile and shook hands. I agreed, just before he and his wife departed, that I would be available if he wanted me.

Like most patients, Harl was nervous and anxious about the prospects of surgery. Unlike most, however, he took control of the situation and decided in a rational, intelligent manner where and when to have the surgery.

Most patients are herded like sheep. Very few are like Harl. Here, in his own words, is his story:

The January sun filtered through the trees as I strode the four blocks from my campus office to Iowa State University's Parks Library. The walk was brisk, partly because the air was chilly, partly because I was in a hurry. The U.S. Department of Agriculture had called me at a meeting in Miami the previous Friday to see if I could go to Poland in February. The unexpected Poland trip meant that I would have to crowd four weeks' work into two, and I was already behind because of the meetings in Florida. So the pace was brisk, and my mind was on how I could cut commitments to leave for Warsaw in just thirteen days.

Suddenly, the focus shifted. As I passed the entrance to LeBaron Hall, I felt tightness in the upper chest. No pain, not even discomfort. Just tightness. Decades of concern about heart problems surfaced, with my inner voice saying, "Harl, that's a dangerous sign. You haven't felt that before."

But another voice was saying, "It's a cold day.

You're inhaling cold air. It's nothing more than a complaint from your lungs." Besides, the tightness disappeared once I arrived at the library, checked out my key counter for the copy machines, and sat down to do my weekly updates for material for my publications. I dismissed the problem, and there was no repeat on the return to my office. What I didn't appreciate then was that the first half of the walk to the library was uphill. Returning, the last half was downhill.

A week later, I walked again to the library to update my agricultural law publications and seminar manuals, which all depend on a relentless outpouring of new developments. I had installed a computer terminal providing electronic access to the new developments on a daily basis, but I still preferred the "hard copy" approach. Besides, I enjoyed the walk to the library. It had been a weekly tradition for more than a decade. And traditions die hard.

The brisk walk on January 29 produced a replay of the January 22 experience. At almost the same spot, the tightness returned, then escalated to mild discomfort. I could feel faint pain. *If this persists, I suppose something should be done,* I thought. *But I'm less than a week away from leaving for Poland. I don't have the time to open that can of worms now.* Besides, my earlier hypothesis of inhaling too much cold air still seemed appropriate. Again, the tightness, discomfort, and pain quickly disappeared in the library. And again, there was no problem walking back to my office.

The following Sunday, February 4, I left for Poland with no thought of cardiac problems. And fortunately, for me, there wasn't the slightest hint of a problem there. We were ferried around in vans and taxis. We ate too much good food high in fats and cholesterol. Pork

154

is the number one meat in Poland, and it's much fatter than American pork. The Poles were going out of their way to feed us fine, rich food.

On the return trip, my Lufthansa flight was rescheduled to enter the United States at John F. Kennedy Airport instead of at Chicago. That necessitated a mad dash with luggage to catch a connecting flight to Chicago. Yet there wasn't a hint of discomfort, even though the stress level easily exceeded my brisk campus walks.

The following Monday, however, on February 19, the same trip across campus brought the pain back again. Full force, with a bit more pain than before. Clearly, I told myself, this problem cannot be ignored much longer. If this persists, I'll have to go to the clinic. But there was catch-up work to do. A pile of work had accumulated during my two-week absence. The problem could wait.

The following Monday, I made the walk with no discomfort whatsoever. Hah! I was right! It was no more than the cold air in my lungs. I promptly forgot the whole thing.

But the next Monday, March 5, it hit again, with even greater force. It couldn't be ignored, and it set me thinking about another recent development. Since 1971, when we moved into our building, I had climbed the stairs to my fourth-floor office rather than taking the elevator. From the rear entrance, where I usually entered, it was ninety steps to the fourth floor. For years, I could dash up the stairs at a brisk clip with a briefcase and an armload of books. But for the last fifteen months, I was more winded when I got to the fourth floor. True, I had put on some weight. And I was getting older. But I began to think that the campus-walk and stair-climbing phenomena were related.

I had to go to the clinic. But I was busy that afternoon, and all day Tuesday and Wednesday. Thursday looked like a possibility. I made a mental note to stop in at the clinic that morning, if the problem persisted. Wednesday night, the chest tightness and pain hit during sex. Weeelll, it's one thing to threaten my walk to the library, even the walk up the back stairs. It's another to threaten my sex life. I would definitely stop at the clinic Thursday morning.

About 8:45 A.M., I sauntered into acute care at McFarland Clinic, a large, well-staffed medical facility in Ames. My personal physician had left Ames a few months earlier, so I decided to take potluck. It turned out to be Dr. James Gohman. I was feeling good, even jaunty. Maybe *cocky* is a better term. I really felt there was probably a simple, innocuous explanation for the discomfort.

We exchanged pleasantries. Bantered good-naturedly. The weight was too high—206 pounds! Unbelievable. I jokingly accused the nurse of not balancing the scale. My blood pressure was fine, even on the low side, at 110 over 70. Pulse was normal. Then she sent me to the EKG lab for an electrocardiogram. The last one had been several years earlier. The new EKG machines are computerized and automatically analyze and print out the results. The operator had some difficulty getting the machine to function. An ice storm had cut off power the night before and had affected the computer. Finally, it functioned and yielded a sheet replete with cardiac squiggles. I couldn't decipher it, but it didn't take much medical insight to read what the computer had printed across the top in bold letters—*abnormal.* Dr. Gohman's immediate reaction was to urge a cardiac catheter procedure—known generally as an angiogram—as soon as possible, preferably the following morning. I demurred with the excuse that "I've got classes at nine and ten A.M. and meetings all afternoon."

Dr. Gohman responded sternly, "If you die tonight, they'll figure out some way to handle your classes."

Reluctantly, I agreed. Dr. Gohman made a phone call and confirmed that Dr. Stark, a cardiologist, could perform the procedure the following morning. As I left Dr. Gohman's office, he said, "By the way, I want you to go straight home, not to the office, and I want you to remain quiet until tomorrow morning." In a final sobering move, he gave me a small bottle of nitroglycerin tablets with instructions to take them if I had chest pain.

Actually, I did go to the office briefly that afternoon. But I walked very slowly, took the elevator, and avoided unnecessary exertion. The nitroglycerin was in my pocket.

At eight o'clock the next morning, I checked into Mary Greeley Medical Center for the cardiac catheter procedure, set for 10:00 A.M. The nurse carefully prepared me for the procedure, physically and emotionally. Large areas of my body were shaved, particularly around the groin. Then she explained that I would be on intravenous solutions to build up water in my body. The procedure involved only a local anesthetic for the groin area, she said, and a small X-ray device would be inserted there and maneuvered up to the heart. A dye solution would be released, flooding my body with dye. "It feels like you're urinating on yourself," she said. And it did. The room would be cool but not uncomfortable, she said, and I would be lying on a very narrow table and could see the monitor as the X-ray device filmed the heart and its vessels.

The release I had to sign for the procedure was sobering. It said that some people suffer strokes and a few die from the procedure. A very few are allergic to the dye and suffer various ill effects.

While waiting to be taken to the cardiac cath procedure room I picked up the *Wall Street Journal.* Inside the main section was a startling story. The FDA had pulled from the market some of the equipment manufactured by one firm for cardiac cath procedures. I mentioned that to the nurse, and she immediately summoned the head of the cardiac cath technical team to check to see if Mary Greeley was using that equipment. It turned out that the word about the equipment involved had been out several weeks, and the offending items had largely disappeared from use. At least, Mary Greeley wasn't using that particular brand.

A few minutes before 10:00 A.M., I was wheeled down to the cath lab and placed on the narrow table. It was firm but not uncomfortably hard, and I was covered with blankets so the cool temperature wouldn't make me uncomfortable. The staff made the procedure as "user-friendly" as possible.

As I lay there awaiting the cardiologist, I gazed around the room. It was a high-tech marvel, with electronic equipment everywhere, some hanging from the ceiling and some that seemed to be rolled in just for the occasion. Finally, Dr. Stark strode in. Within moments, the procedure was under way. It was eerie, with every step proceeding as explained—the entry of the catheter, the release of the dye, and the emergence of the first images on the monitor. It was hard to believe that anyone could thread even a small catheter through my vessels to the heart in such short order. But he did. It seemed Dr. Stark wanted every conceivable angle covered. The machine hovered over my chest, whirred, clanked, and assumed every position imaginable. Then, abruptly, Dr. Stark said, "That's it."

With that, I was wheeled back to my room, totally water-logged with saline solution from the IV. The admonition was to lie perfectly still for the rest of the day. I wasn't to raise an arm or a leg, or even cross my legs. The concern seemed to be that the entry area in the groin might hemorrhage. I dutifully complied.

The water-logged state soon produced a perplexing problem. How does one urinate lying perfectly flat on one's back while being completely still? After several unsuccessful attempts, over an hour or more, with the problem becoming increasingly urgent, I finally mastered the task. Or, should I say, my body managed to overcome its reluctance to cooperate.

About 3:30 P.M. I was greeted by an entourage of distinguished guests—Dr. Stark, the cardiologist; Dr. Gohman; the nurse; and my wife. Dr. Stark led off with a brief, to-the-point summary of the findings. I had very serious blockage of the pipes. Two were 95 percent blocked and another about 60 percent blocked.

What were the options? Again, with characteristic forthrightness, Dr. Stark laid them out: (1) Angioplasty, the balloon procedure, was out of the question. The blockage was too great. The chances of damage to the vessels were too high, and the recurrence rate for angioplasty (30 percent in a year) meant I could be spending a great deal of time in hospitals. (2) The blockage was so extreme that medication wouldn't be effective in reversing the process. (3) I could do nothing and live with enormous uncertainty. I might live two months or ten years. No one could say. (4) I could have bypass surgery. That quick listing of options hit with the force of a ten-ton truck. Cardiac bypass—open-heart surgery—that was for old people! How could I, a mere fifty-six, be a candidate for anything as extreme as that?

There were comforting thoughts: *If you survive the surgery, you'll stand a good chance of full recovery. Your heart is a bit sluggish, but we don't believe it has suffered much, maybe not at all.*

The discussion produced two key questions: (1) What, if anything, should I authorize? (2) Where should it be done? Should I go to the famed heart center in Houston? Or Mayo's? Or Cleveland? Or Iowa City? Or Des Moines? If Des Moines, should I go to Mercy or Methodist?"

Dr. Stark summed up the medical sentiment: If you're facing an exotic problem, go to the place with the most experience with the problem. My surgery, he promised, would be a straightforward procedure. Another physician later called it "dull," another called it a "bread-and-butter" procedure. Dr. Stark said he'd been sending half of his patients to Mercy and the other half to Methodist for about a year and a half. The results were similar, he indicated, but the ones at Methodist seemed to come back feeling a bit better about the surgical experience.

I wasn't prepared to make any decision at that point—about what to have done, if anything, or where to have it carried out. I needed time to think. Dr. Gohman set an appointment for 11:00 A.M. Monday in his office, and the members of the entourage departed—except for my wife.

160

Undoubtedly the most difficult period of the entire process—from the onset of chest discomfort to complete recovery—was the weekend after release from Mary Greeley Medical Center. Even as I rode from the hospital, the questions were weighing on my mind. What should I authorize? Where should I go?

The weekend was not spent in solitude. Indeed, I had hardly arrived at home before the calls and visits commenced. A number of callers reported successful open-heart surgery. George Norris of Ames, an early member of the bypass club, called with a cheery, get well message. My cousin and close friend, David Bryant, called with a reminder that he had bypass surgery at age fifty-seven in 1979 and was continuing to feel good. He left me with what turned out to be a highly important bit of advice: "If you go through with it, keep your mind set on a vision of yourself functioning as you would like to function after surgery. Keep that vision firmly in mind. There will be days when you need that."

Following church on Sunday morning, Charmaine Book, the former head surgical nurse with the Mercy Medical Center team, gave me a rundown on the merits of the Mercy team headed by Dr. Steven Phillips. She recommended Mercy without reservation. Old friends, Ike and Arlene Jutting, called with an offer to visit with their son, who was part of the Mercy technical staff at the time. They did so, and passed on a strong recommendation.

As the weekend came to a close, it was clear that it was concern about the unknown that made the decision difficult. I needed to talk to knowledgeable medical people firsthand.

On Monday morning, Dr. Gohman indicated that

Dr. Stark had made a tentative appointment for 3:30 P.M. that day with the surgical team at Iowa Methodist Medical Center. I asked him to also make an appointment with someone in Iowa City. Within a few minutes, Dr. Gohman had set up a session for Wednesday, March 14, with Dr. Michael Winniford, head of the cardiac catheter laboratory at the College of Medicine in Iowa City.

The appointment Monday afternoon was with two surgeons primarily associated with Iowa Methodist in Des Moines, Dr. Ronald Grooters and Dr. Kent Thieman. Darlene and I arrived at their offices in the Methodist complex shortly before 3:30 P.M. and were advised that they were still in surgery. About twenty minutes later, Dr. Thieman arrived in surgical greens, followed by Dr. Grooters a few minutes later. The discussion was brisk, frank, and candid.

"We've looked at your films and agree bypass is your best option," Thieman said.

He drew a diagram of the heart and associated vessels and explained where the blockages were and how they proposed to install the bypasses. They would use the inner mammary artery if usable, with the rest of the bypass vessels coming from veins in my legs. He explained that, with bypass surgery, the old vessels are left in place and the new vessels are merely grafted on above and below the blockage to permit a full flow of blood to the heart.

How did the team stack up? Dr. Thieman reported that in 1989, Mercy had just under 550 cases, Methodist about 50 fewer. But the Methodist caseload had been spread over fewer surgeons. We discussed the medical school and residency experiences of the Methodist surgeons. All had impressive backgrounds.

162

The youngest, Dr. Robert Schneider, was an Iowa State University graduate who recalled knowing me in his days on the campus in Ames. Dr. Grooters mentioned that he was collaborating on research projects at Iowa State University's College of Veterinary Medicine. He also discussed his ideas for an artificial heart on which some work had been done. I was impressed by the scholarly bent of the group. They were bright, able people with a professional interest in improving performance.

As for statistics, the group seemed quite proud of their postop infection rate—0.16 percent, well under the national average. That was good news. One doesn't need a bout with infection after open-heart surgery. The surgeons said their death rate was about 0.5 percent, well under the national average. They said the low rate could not be taken entirely at face value, explaining that a highly competent surgeon who takes on a lot of difficult cases could have a higher death rate than a less skilled surgeon who takes only routine cases. Nevertheless, their low rate of 0.5 percent was reassuring to me.

During the discussion, a great deal of time was devoted to where the procedure might go wrong. The surgeons explained that a stroke was a possibility. In particular, a stroke could occur because of plaque—the accumulated deposits in the vessels—being dislodged during surgery. Dr. Grooters said that plaque could be loosened by the pumping action of the heart-lung machine when it is hooked up to the aorta. He explained that he had invented a device, still in its experimental stages, for testing for the presence of plaque in the aorta. If plaque is detected, the heart-lung machine is hooked up elsewhere. Other sites are not as good in other ways, but the chance of stroke is lessened. Dr. Grooters said that, to date, forty-three individuals had agreed to participate in the experimental use of the testing device. Of that number, five had showed sufficient evidence of plaque to justify changing the location for hookup of the heart-lung machine. I was impressed with the additional precaution and indicated I wanted to participate if the decision was made to go forward with surgery at Iowa Methodist.

A major concern of mine was that the heart might not restart after surgery. As part of the open-heart surgery procedure, the heart is cooled and idled for several minutes. After the bypass grafts are completed, it is warmed and restarted. *But what if it doesn't restart?*

Dr. Gooters, and Dr. Thieman were very patient in their explanations. Usually, the heart starts right up. Once in a while, an electrical stimulus is needed to restart the organ. Once in a great while, a pacemaker is left in for a couple of hours or so. Once in a great, great while, the pacemaker is left in for a longer period. And once in a great, great, great while, it doesn't start at all. That was sobering, but I was assured that the odds of that happening were exceedingly low, particularly for someone with a reasonably healthy heart.

The surgeons acknowledged that general anesthetic itself creates a small chance of death, but again, the probabilities were low.

Infection of the chest wound is a possibility, but their infection rate was well under a quarter of 1 percent. That seemed like a manageable risk.

Not until a month later did I learn of another potential problem with coronary bypass surgery. In a study at the Long Island Jewish Medical Center, it was reported that 17 percent of coronary bypass patients after surgery had trouble concentrating, remembering new information, and performing mental tasks as quickly as before surgery. Those results would not have tipped the balance against surgery, but they were highly relevant.

I explained to the surgeons that we had an appointment at the medical school in Iowa City on Wednesday; if that went as anticipated, I would like to schedule surgery as soon as possible thereafter, possibly Thursday. Dr. Grooters said that would be fine. They would fit me in whatever day I preferred. He indicated that he would be taking a week off for a skiing vacation, so a Thursday surgery would work fine.

When we walked out of the hospital that evening, I felt a high level of confidence had been established with the surgical team. I am convinced that it is enormously beneficial for the patient to meet with at least the head surgeon, to converse about key concerns, and to gain a measure of confidence in the team. In my own case, I doubt that any other single step contributed more to my peace of mind and feelings of confidence that the correct decisions had been made, both with respect to the procedures authorized and with respect to the location for the surgery. Despite the high-tech nature of medicine today, the human dimension is still vitally important.

One more step remained for me, however—the trip to Iowa City to see Dr. Michael Winniford at the University of Iowa's cardiac catheter laboratory. I took the film from my March 9 cardiac cath procedure at Mary Greeley for him to view.

The trip by automobile to Iowa City took place on a rainy, damp, miserable March day. Darlene rode along. The first forty miles or so passed in total silence. The realization had hit me that morning that I was getting close to a decision. I probably would choose open-heart surgery. And I might not survive. The discussion over the previous several days had been detached. It was almost as if I had been representing a client who was considering bypass surgery, and my task was to ferret out as much information for the client as possible. With a chill, I suddenly realized, *I am the client.*

Somewhere near the Newton exit on Interstate 80 eastbound, I broke the silence.

"We need to talk about what will happen if I don't make it."

That got Darlene's attention instantly. Up to that point, she had been driving. But as soon as the discussion became serious, she wheeled to the side of the road so I could drive and she could take notes. For the rest of the trip and most of the return trip back to Des Moines later that day, the discussion ranged over where I would like to be buried (preferably the Iowa State University Cemetery), how the farm property should be managed, what decisions should be made on retirement accounts and other investments, and where the insurance policies were located. The discussion did nothing to brighten the rainy, dreary day. Indeed, it was a somber trip.

The focus of discussion had produced such a downer that I thought lunch at the Iowa River Power Company in Coralville might help cheer us up. It did. It's a charming place, located in an old power company building on the Iowa River. The food is always excellent. As I made my way around the salad bar, it struck me that this might well be one of the last occasions to eat with reasonable abandon. But the sober realization that vessels were nearly plugged, and were becoming more plugged with each unwise bite, kept my gluttonous instincts in check. I ate moderately and responsibly.

We arrived at the busy Carver Pavilion a few minutes before 1:30 P.M. for the appointment with Dr. Winniford, who was quite young, very bright, and highly articulate. He went through the films from the Ames cardiac cath procedure almost frame by frame, calmly pointing out the vessels involved, the nature and location of the blockages, and the impact on the heart muscle. His conclusion: You really only have two options—do nothing or have bypass surgery. Angioplasty, the balloon procedure, would not be a good choice, and medication would not likely to be successful. That confirmed the diagnoses of Dr. Stark, the cardiologist; Dr. Gohman; and the surgical team at Methodist.

What about where I should have it done?

"It's not likely to be a complicated procedure," Winniford said. "It's a bread-and-butter type of bypass surgery. Nothing about it should be unusual or complicated."

Then he pointed out: "Go to a place where the surgeons are experienced and where the hospital is large enough to have adequate backup facilities."

"What about Mercy or Methodist?"

"Both would be fine choices," he said. "There are small programs around the country I would have some concerns about, but both Methodist and Mercy would do a fine job."

As we walked out of Carver Pavilion, the day was still dreary, the skies were still leaden, but I realized the time had come to make a decision. From a pay phone, I called the surgical group at Methodist.

"I've decided to go ahead with bypass surgery," I said. "If possible, schedule me for admission tonight, as tentatively planned, for surgery tomorrow."

Dinner that evening at Spaghetti Works in Des Moines seemed fleetingly like the last meal for the condemned. But the feelings of confidence from my visit with Dr. Winniford and from the conference with the surgeons crowded out my feelings of doom. Without those visits, I would have been far more apprehensive about surgery.

After a leisurely dinner, we drove up the hill to Methodist and checked in. During the lengthy admission process, our senior pastor from Ames, Rev. Galen Peckham, stopped by for a pastoral call. Finally, around 8:15 P.M., I was escorted to my room.

Our oldest son, Brent, arrived on a plane from Denver that evening and made a brief visit sometime after 10:00 P.M. Clearly, his presence was one of the most buoyant and helpful factors in the entire process. He leans toward being a congenital optimist and casts a happy glow on just about any situation. It was wonderful to have him there on the day of surgery and during my recovery. Dr. Grooters called with several questions and to tell me I would be the lead-off patient, scheduled for 7:30 A.M., March 15.

Because I was under orders to be showered and ready to go by 6:00 A.M., I pondered briefly the long road ahead and switched out the light. Somewhat strangely, I felt a sense of peacefulness that seemed almost bizarre, considering what lay ahead. Surprisingly, there was no fear of the upcoming surgery. But as I told my family, once you have made the two key decisions regarding what procedure to authorize and where to have it done, you need only buckle your seat belt and go along for the ride. It's largely out of your hands from that point on. In retrospect, the only qualifier I would add is the enormous importance of a positive mental attitude.

The wake-up call at 5:30 A.M. jolted me out of a deep, deep sleep. Certainly, the prospect of open-heart surgery hadn't interfered with my slumber. A quick pHisoHex shower and I was ready to go. At 6:00 A.M., the aides came for me. The last thing I recall is the statement: "We'll give you a little anesthetic to start the process."

My next realization, which seemed like only a second later, was the startling return to consciousness after surgery. Usually, after sleep, one feels at least the sensation that some time has passed. In this instance, perhaps because of the depth of the anesthesia, it was as though time had been suspended. It was a bit like being poised at the end of the runway for the takeoff roll one instant, and the next instant waking up on final approach for landing. It was momentarily frightening, and the feelings of fright were compounded by the tubes in my throat and abdomen, the strange, uncomfortable sensation in my chest, and the general realization that several people were gathered around my head, offering encouragement.

In seconds, the feelings of fright subsided as I regained my senses and realized what had happened. I could breathe, swallow with a little difficulty, move my arms and legs, and see the clock on the wall—5:30 P.M. I had been under nearly twelve hours.

One of the things I saw after regaining consciousness was a huge balloon tied to the foot of my bed. Brent had sneaked it into intensive care, and it showed an impish figure with a huge, toothy grin. It read: "This is a 'Get-Well' Balloon—It's Filled with Heal-ium." That provoked a chuckle, even though I scarcely felt like chuckling.

Within minutes, Brent started relating an episode that had caused deep concern, at least among family members, and apparently among the medical team as well. The surgery had gone well, with five bypasses rather than the three originally planned. My heart had been stopped for an hour and thirty-five minutes. It was restarted without the need of electrical stimulus.

But for some unexplained reason my blood pressure crashed on the way from surgery to the coronary intensive care unit. Indeed, it reportedly had fallen from around 120 over 70 to 40 over 30.

The family had been advised: "He's not doing well right now. Dr. Grooters is with him, trying to decide what to do."

After about thirty minutes of administering fluids and medication, my blood pressure returned to normal. Later, two of the three surgeons on the surgical team theorized that it was a problem of low blood supply. As they explained it: during surgery, the body is cooled down, the blood vessels contract, and less blood is needed. When surgery has been completed, the body begins to warm up and the vessels begin expanding, calling for more blood. In my case, the expansion apparently was a bit greater than normal, the blood supply wasn't sufficient, and my system started to close down. Scary.

My first concern after hearing Brent's explanation was that an interruption of blood flow could have caused brain damage. I promptly started testing myself, performing mental mathematical calculations, to see if my brain was functioning properly. I concluded that little, if any, damage had been done. I was immensely relieved. All the way through the period leading up to surgery, my greatest concern was not death—it was that a stroke or other malady would leave me alive but severely impaired. That's clearly the worst of all worlds.

My family later told me that, coming from surgery, I looked like I had visited the gates of hell. My eyes were a sickly green, my skin was ashen, and my face badly bloated. I looked a mess. Amazingly, much of that had disappeared by the time I regained consciousness.

The hospital recovery process was made as "user-friendly" as possible. The nurses, in particular, were wonderfully sensitive. Hospitals genuinely believe in exercise. On Saturday, two days after surgery, I sat on the edge of my bed, and later the same day walked about sixty feet in the corridor with my IV bag dangling from a metal stand rolling along beside me. The doctor had removed the tubes from my throat and abdomen. The tube down my throat had been particularly offensive and had left my throat a bit sore.

With elimination of the tubes and IV, I became more mobile. On Sunday, I walked seven times around the heart ward—something over a half a mile. Monday was the turnabout day. Bodily functions hadn't returned completely to normal, and the effects of anesthesia were still very real. I had a general feeling that my system was thoroughly disgruntled at being so completely invaded. But on Monday, I was decidedly better, and I celebrated by taking a shower, putting on sweats, and walking fourteen times around the heart ward. I also started cardiac rehabilitation, a supervised exercise program.

Monday also was the day I encountered persistent throat irritation and coughing. Among the greatest enemies of a bypass patient are coughing and sneezing. Both rack the chest, intensifying the surgery wound pain by a factor of at least ten and making one wonder if there is any greater punishment. In my case, the throat tube had left an irritation that seemed to trigger coughing spasms after talking for an hour or so. And as my friends and acquaintances know, I love to talk if anyone is around. So on Monday, I was sipping ice water, sucking on throat lozenges, and hoping the cough would go away. Belatedly, I realized that my sweats were keeping my body heat elevated, which seemed to exacerbate the coughing. Once I changed to lightweight pajamas, the coughing virtually stopped.

The first several nights after surgery were highly peculiar experiences, to say the least. Sleep was fitful and very light. A couple of nights, I was convinced I didn't sleep at all. When I did sleep, my mind conjured up strange sensations and bizarre circumstances. One night, after a discussion on stress, the message from sleep was, "Stress is like acid being poured on your incisions; your body won't heal until you deal with the stress in your life." That was unsettling, to say the least. Another night, I was awakened several times as my roommate was being ministered to by the nurses. Each time the light came on, I developed excruciating pains in my lower back. As soon as the light went off and the nurses left the room, the pain would disappear. Once, when the discomfort was unusually severe, I called for the nurse and tried to explain my plight. It was obvious that the nurse thought I had been dreaming.

Monday, March 19, was such an upbeat day that I started lobbying for release. I had been told that seven days was the usual confinement after open-heart surgery, and I doubted that I would make it on Tuesday. But with a little prodding, maybe I could get out on Wednesday. The response from the cardiologist on Monday was a blank stare. On Tuesday, I renewed my plea and was told, "Maybe, just maybe, on Wednesday; it all depends on how you get along."

Tuesday, I was up to two miles of walking plus supervised exercise. I was feeling great, perhaps too great, it seemed to me. My bodily functions were back to normal. I felt on top of the world. Briefly, I considered an unauthorized excursion to the snack bar several floors below, but I realized the transmitters in the monitors we wore had a very short range, and the nurses' station would know as soon as I left the seventh floor. A bank of monitors at the nurses' station maintained a steady portrayal of our cardiac performance.

A highlight of each day was the arrival of the day's mail. I received well over three-hundred cards and letters. Another highlight was the arrival of plants and flowers. By the time of my dismissal, my room looked like a converted greenhouse. There is no doubt that cards, letters, and plants cheer the patient and spur recovery. Plants and flowers are tangible evidence of life and convey a message of high hope to the patient.

A significant event during hospital recovery was the daily lecture on some relevant topic—diet, exercise, and stress were the major subjects. As expected, the dietitian came down hard on fats and cholesterol. After that session, I was ready to embrace seafood, to eschew

173

butter, cream, and cheese, to strip skin from chicken and turkey, and to cut my consumption of fatty red meat to zero. Lean cuts were acceptable, but bacon and sausage—two of my favorites—were on the taboo list. Ironically, that day *The Des Moines Register* carried a story about the state legislature excoriating Des Moines' mayor for signing a proclamation urging consumers to ease off red meats for a day. The mayor's language seemed totally consistent with what I had been hearing from health care and dietary professionals for several days.

My concern about diet was real. A dozen or so years earlier, my cholesterol level had been observed above the 300 level. With some dietary modification I had managed to get it down to the 240-260 range. During my annual physical in February 1989, the cholesterol level had been 265. Doctors like to see the level below 200.

Moreover, high cholesterol levels tend to run in my family. My father had an observed level of more than 400 two years before dying of a heart attack at age seventy. My mother, almost eighty now, has a slightly elevated cholesterol level. Her father died of a massive heart attack at age sixty-five. My two sisters have cholesterol levels similar to mine. My older brother, now deceased but not because of heart problems, suffered angina and underwent angioplasty at age fifty-two.

Finally, on Tuesday, Dr. Schneider agreed to sign my release, and later that day one of the nurses clipped the staples holding the incision together in my right leg. Four of the five grafts had come from the inside of my right leg, with the incision above my knee. Despite the fact that many open-heart patients say leg pain is

174

the worst pain suffered, I would not have known the incision was there had I not seen it. It healed perfectly, with no infection, and almost no discomfort.

On Wednesday morning, I was ready to go home. I showered, exercised, packed my bag, and said good-byes all around. Finally, after one final test, the aides whisked me back to the seventh floor and then down to the first floor with my belongings and enough flowers and plants to start a floral business. Free at last. Never had the air seemed sweeter or the sun shone brighter. There may have been nicer days than March 21, 1990, but I am certain I have never seen a more beautiful one, nor do I believe I'll ever see a nicer day in the future. It was wonderful to be out.

Shopping for Heart Care

Driving to and from work with the radio on, I frequently hear ads for the competing hospital's heart program. They describe themselves as the area's leader in heart surgery, and I have to admit it makes my blood boil. My lips start moving and I start to swear: "Damn! There they go again!"

It's the American way, I guess. Americans are informed and/or fooled every day by slick advertising. Buy this. Use that. So I shouldn't be surprised that hospitals use the news media or resort to advertising to build their reputation and images. Iowa Methodist, the hospital where I perform surgery, does it, too.

The thing is, we have consumer guides in this country for just about everything—cars, appliances, tires, home computers, you name it. You don't have to depend on the slick ads if you don't want to. But do you know where to turn for advice when shopping for heart care? Of course not! There are no consumer guides for cardiologists or heart surgeons, no guides rating hospital units on a one- to five-star scale, although the state of Iowa is making an experimental attempt with Medis Group Two, available in April 1992 to provide "quality" data. This will be just raw data and not necessarily reliable information.

Needless to say, heart care is a lot more vital than choosing a car, a stereo, or paint for your house. Yet the average American has no handy heart-care guide to help make care choices and decisions. In many cases, people may just rely on the advice of their family physicians. But the fact is, many primary care physicians do not have the information they would need to find the best cardiac care. It could be that *they* are relying on the advertising and public relations they hear, or they may be referring patients to a particular hospital simply because it's the one they're associated with or the one where they trained. Many referrals are made because of loyalties or business relationships, not necessarily quality. Most people assume their doctor knows best. They assume that their doctor is sending them to one of the best places for care. The fact of the matter is that many times their doctors don't really know. In fact, even I don't know for sure where our heart program stands in comparison to other heart programs around the country. So what do you do if you don't want to simply follow the Pied Piper of marketing and public relations? What do you do if you want to rely on more than one doctor's referral? What do you do if you want to make an intelligent choice?

First, you should be aware that in the United States you're going to get good, top-notch heart care from 95 percent of the cardiologists and surgeons. What *you* want to do is eliminate the few exceptions, and then find the best heart care available.

Here are the things I would do if I were faced with the decision, and I honestly believe they will serve you well:

Start with the hospital first. How long has the hospital had a heart program? If it's less than five years, it may not be the best place for you. Check to see if it had at least 100 heart surgery patients in the first year and at least 250 by the fifth year. The 250 surgeries per year, a reflection of commitment and experience, ought to be your minimum for all hospitals.

If it's below that level, there is an increased chance that the institution is not yet the top-quality heart-care center you would want to go to.

Be inquisitive! Ask the surgeon, cardiologist, or nurse about the hospital. (Sometimes nurses are a little more truthful.) There's one question that I think is very important: Does your hospital have a postgraduate training program in the basics of surgery, medicine, pediatrics, or family practice? I think a hospital should have at least three of those four, including the surgery and medicine programs, to qualify as your heart-care hospital. At the very least, if a hospital is not involved in the upper-level training of doctors, you ought to consider that a mark against it when it comes to heart surgery or other complicated procedures. Why? Let me give you a real life-and-death example, one from my own experience at Iowa Methodist in Des Moines.

It was about midnight when I finished a five-vessel bypass on a very nice, well-preserved gray-haired woman. It had been a long, hard day in the operating room, beginning about 6:00 A.M. with breaks totaling only two or three hours during the eighteen-hour day. I was exhausted but content. The last operation had gone very well. I'd stayed with the woman for an hour and a half after the surgery. She was stable, doing very well. Her blood pressure was fine. Her heart rhythm was normal. The lab tests and X rays looked good, and she was not bleeding from her chest tubes. No problems. The woman was doing fine, so I went home and was asleep as soon as my head hit the pillow around 1:00 A.M.

Just five minutes later, however, the phone rang.

"Now what?" I assumed I would have to verbally hold a nurse's hand for a few minutes, and then back to sleep. I couldn't have been more wrong. Over the phone, loud and clear, came a frantic scream: "We need you! Right now!"

The woman had just dumped massive amounts of blood from her chest drainage tubes. No blood pressure. Without immediate help, she would die. I bolted out of bed, my heart pounding, feeling the way I would if a car suddenly pulled out in front of me on the highway. Damn! I knew I had to calm myself. I needed to think calmly and rationally and do the right things. This woman's life depended on that. Several seconds of silence passed as I tried to collect my thoughts. I had no idea what had happened to this woman. Something had popped loose somewhere. That didn't matter now. I needed an edge or a whole lot of luck to save her. It would take me ten or fifteen minutes to speed to the hospital, and by that time she'd be dead. I barked out orders to get blood and an Adrenalin drip started right away. The edge. The edge. What about the edge? Of course!

"Call the surgical resident! Tell him to open her chest! Now! Right there in the coronary unit."

I shouted like a lieutenant in battle. I jumped into jeans and a T-shirt, dressing as I dashed out the door, then roared to the hospital, speeding all the way. At the same time, a sleepy resident shuffled into the intensive care unit, rubbing his eyes.

"What's wrong?" he asked with very little urgency.

The nurse's reply jolted him wide awake: "Dr. Grooters wants you to open this woman's chest right now!"

The nurses had the emergency standby tray of chest instruments and surgical gloves ready and waiting. The resident had helped me and other heart surgeons many times and had occasionally opened and closed heart patients. This was his ultimate test, and he instinctively went into action, proceeding as we had discussed during chest-training sessions. He took scissors to cut the woman's stitches, then wire cutters to snip the wires holding her breastbone together. He inserted the retractor and opened her chest to gain exposure of her compressed, weakly beating heart. It was almost empty and had collapsed like a punctured football. Relieving the pressure from blood around her heart brought her pressure up to 50, but it plunged again as the bleeding resumed.

When I arrived, about fifteen minutes after the call, I found the resident by the woman's side, blood all over himself and the patient. He looked at me and shook his head. He had kept her alive for the fifteen minutes, but he thought the patient was lost. She didn't have a heartbeat, and his hand massage of the heart wasn't bringing her back.

Together, we explored the heart and found the bleeding point. A vessel clip had popped off the vein graft, leaving a large hole in the graft and causing massive bleeding. Quickly, we grasped the break with our forceps to stop the bleeding. We kept pumping her heart with our hands. More blood arrived, and slowly her pressure came back up. Then it was back to the operating room to clean up the mess and put her back together again.

She walked out of the hospital nine days later. If the budding surgeon hadn't been there, on the spot, she never would have made it. I could relate countless similar situations, instances where a patient would have died if a resident hadn't been there to provide immediate emergency care and the hours of postop attention that it would be physically impossible for the attending staff to provide. Yes, residents make mistakes now and then, but that is more than offset by the help they provide during training in their specialty.

What hospital would I go to? Give me one with a postgraduate training program and an established heart program performing at least 250 surgeries a year.

But that's just the first step. Now you must choose your surgeon. At the very least, you want to check his qualifications and track record. You can do that with some pretty simple questions:

Are you certified by the American Board of Thoracic Surgery? Virtually every surgeon is, but you might as well make sure. Don't be satisfied with anything less or anything else.

How many years of heart surgery experience do you have? I would avoid any surgeon who is part of a team with less than five years' experience. In the early days of heart surgery, patients had to take surgeons with less experience. Today, there is absolutely no reason to go to a group whose senior members have less than five years' experience.

How many open-heart surgeries do you perform a year? Again, if a team (not the hospital) is not doing 250 cases a year, avoid it.

Here are some more specific questions you might want to ask when shopping for a surgeon:

1. *What is your overall mortality rate for bypass patients?* The question is not foolproof because some surgical teams handle more difficult cases than others. If a team's mortality rates are extremely low, it may mean the team is being very selective and taking only easy cases. If your case isn't so easy, or develops unexpected complications, they may not be the best

team to handle it. So let me give you the mortality rate guidelines I would use in selecting a surgical team, with the cautionary note that they are based on my observations, not scientific study:

In my opinion, mortality rates for a heart surgery team ought to be somewhere from 3 percent to 6 percent. If the rate is below 3 percent, it may mean the surgeons are very, very good, but it's more likely that they are selecting very easy cases and not taking patients with very serious problems who would benefit the most from surgery. In fact, surgeons with a very low mortality rate may be performing surgery on people who don't really need surgery. A low mortality rate of below 3 percent is almost too good to be true.

On the flip side, if the team's rate is above 6 percent, the team may be handling very difficult cases above its capabilities or it may be taking too many "hopeless" cases for some reason. There are people who shouldn't go to surgery because they can't be helped or they're going to die anyway. We as surgeons should have enough compassion to let them die in dignity and not to fool them into believing they can be saved through surgery. Finally, the team's mortality rate may be high simply because it doesn't perform surgery very well. I believe this may be the case in about 5 percent of the nation's programs, but again I have no scientific study to prove it, just a feeling based on observation.

If a surgeon says he can't tell you his group's mortality rate for a certain type of surgery, be wary. My partners and I could tell you because we have all of our surgery data in our computer system. For example, in our program, if you are fifty-five years old and need elective bypass surgery, the mortality rate is less than 0.5 percent. On the other hand, if you are seventy-five and need a redo, emergency bypass operation, the mortality rate is about 30 percent. When we mix all of our cases together, our overall mortality rate is somewhere between 3.5 and 4 percent, based on the records of 4,000 patients kept in our computer since 1978. *That is the kind of information a prospective surgical team ought to be able to provide.*

2. *What is your wound infection rate?* Wound infections after surgery are very serious and extremely hard on patients. After heart surgery, they occur in the breastbone, or sternum. The bone does not tolerate infection very well, and may be lost. A great many people end up in the hospital for two to four very painful months because of postoperative infection. It's not something to be taken lightly.

What should the infection rate be? Our team, over a course of ten years, had a sternal infection rate of 0.16 percent. World literature reports rates among various surgical teams ranging from 0.4 percent to 8 percent. Any surgeon or surgical team with an infection rate greater than 1 percent would not touch me. I have studied this scientifically and can tell you without qualification that a surgeon can keep his infection rate below 1 percent with good surgery techniques.

3. *What is your postoperative bleeding rate?* Bleeding after surgery is basically a nuisance for the heart surgeon. It's expensive for the insurance company. And it may be life-threatening for the patient. At the very least, it exposes the patient to potentially dangerous blood products. Ideally, postoperative bleeding requiring a return to surgery should occur in no more than 3 percent of a surgical team's cases. I've heard rumors of prominent programs around the country with postoperative bleeding rates as high as 10 percent.

Large programs with heavy schedules need to move from one surgery to the next as quickly as possible. They take care of the surgeries, and then handle the bleeding patients at the end of the schedule. *No way!* Surgeons need to take the time to make sure all potential bleeding sites are as dry as possible. In my opinion, we should not remove patients from the operating rooms unless bleeding is under control. If a surgeon's return to the operation room for bleeding is greater than 3 percent, don't subject yourself to his care. Look for someone else.

4. *What is your perio-operative infarction rate (heart attack rate during surgery)?* The rate should be no more than 2 to 3 percent for elective bypass cases. Many elements go into preserving the heart during surgery, and much controversy exists on how to measure heart damage. The 2 to 3 percent figure I'm talking about is based on the electrocardiogram after surgery. A rate based on enzymes in the blood (a much more sensitive test) would be much higher, perhaps 8 to 10 percent, but the value of the enzyme count after surgery is an issue of considerable debate.

5. *What is your perio-operative stroke rate for patients under sixty five?* The answer here should be 1 percent or less. For patients over 70, the stroke rate is 4 to 10 percent. In most cases, the surgeon has very little control over the strokes that do occur, but we should be able to control strokes more effectively as our knowledge of stroke causes and how to deal with them improves. My partners and I are very close to solving this problem and will try to publish our findings in a professional journal once they look reasonable or are proven.

After wading through the statistics, you need to

examine your impression and feelings about the surgeon. A surgeon's attitude and bedside manner are important. If you are at ease with your surgeon, your chances of coming through surgery in good shape are improved. Anxiety adds stress to your heart by increasing the body's adrenaline level, elevating your blood pressure, and increasing the resistance of your blood vessels. If the surgeon can sit and talk with you, can make you feel comfortable without being condescending, you can be reasonably sure that he's not condescending to the people he works with, either, and that he probably works efficiently and harmoniously with his team. On the other hand, if he stands over you or talks down to you, telling you what you need to have done with little empathy or feeling, he'll probably be a prima donna in the operating room.

These things ought to be important to you. You want a surgeon who is comfortable with his job, who conducts his complicated surgery in a relaxed, efficient, stress-free environment. You don't want an overbearing ogre working with an emotionally strained team in something as critical as open-heart surgery. When an emergency or sudden change develops, you want a quick, efficient, harmonious unit. You don't want an inhibited, scared team that is slow to react. So don't discount "bedside manner." It's a factor that could save your life.

While you're asking questions, observe the doctor. Is he relaxed and open? Does he listen to your concerns and explain your alternatives? Does he take time to explain his answers thoroughly? Or does he act offended that you would question him? Is he short and abrupt? Does he seem to be in a hurry? He may not be able to answer all of your questions, but you can get a gut feeling about him.

Can he provide you with computerized statistics outlining his surgical history? Can he explain his failure rate? Excuse me for repeating myself, but I cannot stress this too much: Take a very close look at postoperative infection rates and other complications. They are among your best indicators of quality, if the surgeon can quickly and honestly give you *his* statistics. You absolutely do not want to go to a hospital or a surgeon with a high mortality rate or a high infection rate.

Remember, these are the guidelines I would use: An overall death rate of no more than 6 percent, an elective surgery death rate of 1 percent or less, a sternal infection rate of well under 1 percent, and a take-back bleeding rate of 3 percent or less.

Finally, at the risk of repeating myself again: Don't do what most people do. Listen to your family physician, but don't automatically follow his or her advice. Don't automatically obey a referral to one particular cardiologist or surgeon. Don't automatically go to your favorite hospital. They may be the best available, but then again, they may not be. They may be the most aggressive in going after patients. They may have the best public relations.

Keep telling yourself that you have a right to more than one opinion. If a doctor, any doctor, resists a second opinion, then maybe you ought to step back and think. Maybe this is not the doctor you want.

It's a nice little acid test: "I'd like to have a second opinion." If he says, "Fine," you can probably trust him. If he acts arrogant or tries to block it, that ought to be a warning sign.

When you ask the question, the physician should typically say, "Fine. Do you know who you want to see? If so, I'll call and arrange for a visit. If you don't, I would suggest Dr. So-and-so. He's respected, and he'll give you a good, honest opinion."

Remember, it's your life. It's your heart. It's your time here on earth. When it comes to something as important as heart surgery, don't take your friend's word for it, don't necessarily take your doctor's word for it. It's up to you.

Risk Factors and Remedies

He was a lawyer and businessman in a medium-size Iowa town, a man on the go looking for happiness through wealth and success, trying to make it big, leading a high-pressure life full of stress and complications. He owned a bank, until it went into receivership. He used to go three, maybe four days without sleep, then sleep thirty-six hours. He chain-smoked. He lost $100,000 in a high-risk business venture. He was divorcing his wife, his marriage a casualty of his search for happiness. The night he blew (dissected) his aorta, the great trunk artery emerging from the top of his heart, he was in Des Moines with his girlfriend, searching for happiness, looking for relief from his pressure and stress.

I was just sitting down to dinner when I got the news over the phone from the trauma surgeon on call: "Ron, have I got a nice one for you, a forty-six-year-old man with a dissected aorta."

The man had gone to Methodist in a cold sweat with severe abdominal pain—piercing, unrelenting pain, the kind that generates screaming and waves of vomiting and nausea,the kind that makes one feel he's in hell, the kind that no pain shot will relieve. The emergency room physician and trauma surgeon had been alert enough to suspect something much more serious than indigestion or abdominal blockage. A chest CAT scan revealed what they feared: The man's aortic wall was sheared in two like two thin sheets of wet tissue paper. He could die any minute.

188

I drove hard to the hospital, pushing my car and my own blood pressure to the limit. We rushed him to the operating room and started cutting. Inside the man's chest cavity, we found the effects of years of hard living. His lungs were black as carbon paper from smoking, but the immediate problem had been caused by long-term high blood pressure that had weakened, and finally dissected, the wall of the aorta. We see three, maybe four similar cases a year, out of more than five-hundred surgeries. This man was a bloody mess when we cut him open. Blood all over the place. The damaged aorta was buried in clotted blood and was hard to find, but I knew somewhere the weakened aorta could suddenly rupture and blow right in my face. We were lucky. We applied clamps at both ends to cut the blood flow, found the damage, and replaced the section of bad artery with an artificial artery of woven Dacron tubing. The trick was to sew the tubing into softened, damaged tissue without leaving holes that could cause massive bleeding after the repairs. It took careful, methodical insertions of the needle so as not to cut any of the tissue. After four hours of surgery, he was "fixed."

After two weeks, he was still on a ventilator. His smoke-damaged lungs couldn't keep him alive without the help of a respirator. He was wild. He couldn't understand what had happened. We had to tie him down so he wouldn't hurt himself. He looked more like a prisoner than a patient strapped to his bed. We had to sedate him, almost to the point of paralysis, and then ventilate him to keep him alive. Slowly, his postop psychotic behavior mellowed and he returned to a normal mental condition. His lungs began functioning, too, but he was still in critical condition two weeks after the surgery.

189

What happened to this man? Could all of this have been prevented? Definitely! Proper control of his blood pressure would have been a start. An end to the chain-smoking, drinking, eating excessively rich food, and working long, stressful hours would have helped, too. Modifying these self-destructive behaviors would have made all the difference in the world.

This man knew he needed to change his life, but he was out of control. His spirit was out of control, and it was affecting his body. It almost killed him, and he's not out of the woods as I relate his story.

I see a lot of patients like this lawyer, people who have lived their lives on the go, with no thought of what they're doing to themselves. Their lungs are black with smoke. They're obese. Their arteries are clogged with globs of yellow fat from steaks, eggs, and ice cream. Their hearts are enlarged, with stiff, thick walls, from years of fighting high blood pressure.

When people come to see me with something to fix, they have forgotten how they've lived the fifteen, thirty, or fifty years. They have forgotten about the life on the go, go, go. They have forgotten about the smoke in their lungs, the greasy food in their mouths. They don't remember how they have abused their bodies, year after year, with no thought of the cumulative effects, of what it will do to them, how it will catch up to them.

There is only one risk factor we cannot change, and that is genetics. The others can be modified to prevent, or at least slow, high blood pressure, coronary artery plaque buildup, and heart disease.

Smoking is the most obvious risk factor. It is, without a doubt, the most deadly legal habit. I'm still puzzled—no, amazed—that people don't avoid smoking in the first place, knowing full well that it's a habit that can kill you, knowing that once they start they may not have the strength to stop. Smoking kills hundreds of thousands of people every year. Cut out smoking and you can clear your lungs and lower your blood pressure.

Combine smoking with fatty foods and you'll increase your weight and clog your arteries, raising your blood pressure even more. Americans consume 40 percent of their calories in fat, contributing significantly to the need for 300,000 bypass surgeries a year. In Japan, where people get 15 to 20 percent of their calories from fat, there are just 3,000 bypass surgeries a year in a population half as large as that of the United States.

Mix stress in with the cigarettes and fat, and you're on your way to my operating table. If you're lucky, you'll make it before you suffer a heart attack and die. Enlarged hearts thickened and stiffened from years of high blood pressure don't tolerate heart attacks very well. Many don't tolerate them at all. They turn to masses of red mush that refuse to pump. *Don't stop now—keep reading this!*

If you want to see the way we live today, go out to the freeway and watch people drive. Watch the intense drivers, all trying to get there five minutes earlier when five minutes later wouldn't have made much difference. Or go to a restaurant and watch people eat. Thirty to fifty percent of the people you see will be overweight, and they'll be eating enough at one sitting to sustain many people in other countries for two or three days. Eat a hamburger, fries, and a malt, and you're getting lots of fat and cholesterol with 1,200 calories—two-thirds of your daily caloric needs at one meal, and more fat and cholesterol to clog your coronary arteries. We

191

ought to cut meat consumption in half, and we ought to be disciplined enough to eat more fresh fruits and vegetables. Put just one pat of butter on that baked potato instead of three. If you have a roll, don't use butter. If you have to snack, eat carrots and celery. It's not that complicated to cut fat intake, to cut your portions in half. The point is, you don't have to stay in the fast lane to surgery. You can quit smoking. You can start exercising. You can reduce or eliminate high-cholesterol, fatty food, cut back on salt, caffeine, and alcohol. You can slow the pace of your life and find peace and enjoyment in what you have instead of constantly seeking more. All of these steps will improve your cardiovascular health and help keep your weight and blood pressure where they belong. Even hereditary factors can be modified. Hereditary high blood pressure and blood lipid problems can be controlled with medication.

But you have to heal yourself. A surgeon can fix things for a while, can give you a few more years, but he can't heal you. He can't take you off your self-destructive course. Certain emotions—greed, anger, envy, fear—are bad for the heart. Contentment, forbearance, and consideration for others are good for the heart.

The Iowa businessman knew before the surgery that he needed to change his life. He knew he was out of control, but he didn't have the will to do anything about it. His spirit was sick and it had affected his body. He has the will to control his life today, but he found it the hard way.

I saw him two weeks after he was released from the hospital. He came in for a checkup and a chest X ray. His blood pressure was under control, through medica-

192

tion. His wounds from the surgery were healed. More important, his attitude was healed. He had slowed his pace. He was more content. He confessed to me how dangerous his life-style had been and openly expressed disbelief at what he had been doing to himself. He had given up cigarettes, and he told me that he had vowed to himself to get his life back on track. But his chest scar remains, and he has only about a 60 percent chance to live five years. Most men his age have a 98 percent chance. He's reformed, but he can't undo the damage accumulated over the past twenty-five years.

Just like the Iowa businessman, we are all on this earth for a few brief moments, and then we pass on, but I cannot imagine that when people say, "Well, ya gotta die of something," deep down inside they really mean it. I often sense it is more a feeling of hopelessness plus, I believe, selfishness. Think about it. With such thinking, you are not only depriving yourself of good health, you are hurting those close to you and everyone else in society. You don't believe it? Try this on for size:

You smoke. "I want a cigarette now, and any time I want one I should have one," you say to yourself. In health terms, what are you doing? You're killing yourself. In societal terms, what are you doing? *You're placing a burden on others.* How much of a burden? First, your life is shortened by an average of eighteen years, if you're a heavy smoker. "So what?" you ask. Well! that may be eighteen years of productive life. Gone. If your annual salary is $25,000, that's $450,000 over eighteen years. Don't stop there. Multiply that by everyone who smokes in this country. Say it's 40 million people. Now what is the figure? Over eighteen years, it's almost $9 trillion! Let's keep going.

Before all you smokers die, many of you will be disabled and nonproductive. Add another $2 trillion. You'll need medical care for emphysema, heart disease, and other smoking-related ailments. Add that cost. Add the disability cost paid by insurance companies while you're in ill health. Add all the time you'll cost your employer. Add the damaged health to those around you. And the fires accidentally set. And finally, add your cigarette cost. Yes, your meager habit of $600 to $1,000 a year is costing this society trillions of dollars. Your spouse pays for your habit. Your children pay. Society pays. They all pay for years and years and years. You don't just owe it to yourself to quit, you owe it to all of us!

I recall a verse I saw on a calendar once, a quote from the Zoroastrian Scriptures: "Doing good to others is not a duty. It's a joy, for it increases your own health and happiness." Not smoking is doing good to others. Give up any of your unhealthy habits, and you're doing good to others.

There are ten risk factors related to heart disease. Some you can influence by correcting bad habits. Others you have to live with: (1) family history, (2) smoking, (3) high blood pressure (hypertension), (4) obesity, (5) high cholesterol and fats in the blood, (6) diabetes, (7) type A personality, (8) age, (9) gender, and (10) previous heart attack and/or bypass surgery.

I'll explain briefly how each factor can affect you, and how you need to react to it. Whole articles and even books have been written about each topic, but hopefully these brief descriptions will help you understand the factors that contribute to your risk of heart disease:

Family History

Obviously you don't have anything to say about who your parents are. You can't change your entry into the world. Yet this is one of the most important factors in the development of coronary heart disease. A common response to this is one of resignation: "Well, so what? I can't do anything about it." Yes you can. And you should. Keep these three ideas in mind:

1. If you have a parent, grandparent, sister, uncle, or brother who has died of a heart attack, it is even more important for you to minimize your other coronary risk factors. A good, low-fat diet, no smoking, and blood pressure control are of paramount importance. If you don't control the other risk factors, you will accelerate your genetic tendency for severe heart disease.
2. Your children, who may be genetically vulnerable to heart disease, will benefit from your influence, teaching, and example. Plaquing and hardening of the arteries starts in the teens and early twenties. If you, as a parent, teach your children to accept and eat a low-fat diet, at least most of the time, you will be giving them a precious gift, one that can make a tremendous difference later in their lives.
3. Your father had a heart attack at fifty-five. Now you are that age. *Do not ignore* feelings or symptoms of heart disease—chest pain, shortness of breath, indigestion with or after exercise. You should consider treadmill tests

every two years, even if you have no symptoms. Blockages of the arteries can be detected and treated successfully in most cases. Do not avoid diagnosis or treatment because of a feeling of hopelessness or a fear of the costs. With treatment, you can remain healthy and productive. If symptoms are ignored, the cost may be a severe disability or your life.

Smoking

I would like to say, "*Stop smoking!*" and say no more, but I will be a little more scientific and explain how smoking affects the heart, especially if you have coronary heart disease.

The major drug in cigarettes is nicotine. It, along with other substances, triggers a cascade of physiological reactions in your blood vessels. Here is a list:

1. Smoking raises your low-density "bad" cholesterol level, the one that causes arterial plaque buildup, while lowering your "good" high-density hypoprotein cholesterol (HDL-c). This "good" cholesterol is very efficient at tying up the "bad" cholesterol in the bloodstream, and possibly preventing the buildup of plaque in your arteries.
2. Smoking increases your heart rate and blood pressure by stimulating the production and release of adrenaline-like substances from your adrenal glands. This causes the blood vessels to "squeeze down," or narrow, thus

raising your blood pressure and adding to your heart's work load.

3. Nicotine causes the coronary arteries to narrow and spasm, depriving the heart of its normal supply of oxygen and possibly inducing severe heart attack or damage to your heart, especially if you have plaque buildup in your arteries.

4. Smoking makes the platelets, the particles in the blood that promote clotting when needed, more prone to stick together. This "clotting" tendency increases the chances of a clot forming in the coronary vessels or brain vessels, which could cause a heart attack or a stroke.

5. Other clotting substances are increased by smoking, too, increasing the possibility that your blood will clot too quickly.

6. The lining of your blood vessels can be irritated, and even injured, by smoking. This, too, can increase the chances of a dangerous clot formation. Stop smoking and the risk of a heart attack or stroke from clotting will, in all likelihood, be reduced over time by about 20 percent.

7. Smokers have more "silent" episodes of heart ischemia, a condition in which your heart does not get enough blood or oxygen and is damaged without any chest pain or other warning signs.

8. Smoking increases the free fatty acids in your blood that promote the buildup of plaque in your blood vessels.

9. Smoking causes some heart medications to

be metabolized very rapidly, limiting their effectiveness or eliminating them before they have a chance to help you.

10. For fertile women, simultaneous smoking and use of oral contraceptives multiplies the risk of each, creating a dangerous possibility of heart attack, even if there are no plaque buildups or blockages.

Remember that the damage from smoking is slow, steady, insidious, and persistent. The effects are reversible, but it may take five years before you realize the full benefits of kicking your habit.

If people would stop smoking, we probably would see a 30 to 50 percent decrease in heart surgery or heart procedures like angioplasty. Stop smoking and you may hurt my business, but you won't hurt my feelings. In fact, if you want to make both of us feel good, save your smoking money and give what you save to your favorite charity. It will be good for your body and soul.

Hypertension (high blood pressure)

What is this condition? First, you need to know what your blood pressure should be. As a young to middle-aged adult, the upper limits are 130 millimeters of mercury (Hg) for the systolic component and 90 millimeters Hg for the diastolic component. Anything higher in either reading is hypertension. We are all hypertensive at times. During exercise, anxiety, or excitement, our blood pressure can go up, but it should return to normal after a few minutes when we return to a baseline of physical activity or emotional normalcy. If it does not return to normal after a few minutes, you may have the beginning of hypertension.

What is so dangerous about this condition? After all, most people suffer few, if any, immediate symptoms. The danger lies in long-term complications, which usually surface in the fourth or fifth decade of life and increase with age. What are the complications and why do they surface? First, the heart muscle must work much harder when it's pumping against increased pressure. Your biceps will do the same if you "pump iron." They grow big and strong. So it is with the heart. It grows big and strong. So what? That's good, isn't it? But there are limits to the size of the heart. If it grows too big, it becomes inefficient. The muscle cells of the heart get in each other's way, so to speak. Your heart will start to lose blood supply and demand more oxygen. Some muscle cells may die, putting more of a load on the remaining cells. Enlarged hearts do not adjust to, or survive, a heart attack caused by a blocked artery nearly as well. Eventually, an enlarged heart will fail. It is called congestive heart failure.

Second, your blood vessels don't function as well with high blood pressure. Fat and cholesterol accumulate more rapidly on the interior walls, creating blockages, and the walls of the vessels may weaken from the pressure, either thinning out and becoming saclike (aneurysms), or suddenly dissecting, or splitting, into two thin layers like wet tissue paper. Both of these conditions can cause a sudden rupture and fatal bleeding. A swift, painless way to go, perhaps, but why die so young? Why not stay healthy, happy, and productive?

Third, the vessels in your brain can stand the pressure only so long before one ruptures, causing a stroke. Not such a pleasant way to go, especially since you can suffer substantially diminished mental and physical capacity long before death.

Fourth, the kidney vessels don't like the pressure, either. They react by narrowing themselves. Gradually, this narrowing becomes permanent. Kidney cells are lost, and blood pressure rises even more to compensate for the deficit. Eventually you suffer kidney failure. Then you need dialysis or a transplant.

Why not help us prevent high blood pressure, if possible? Stick around longer, and help all of us save health care dollars. Do yourself a favor, take your body for a checkup just half, or even a fourth, as often as you take your car in for service. See your doctor, beginning at age forty, maybe every two or three years. Have your blood pressure checked. If it is high, you may need a low-salt diet and/or medication to control the pressure. If medication doesn't help, the doctor may look for causes, which occasionally can be corrected with surgery.

Obesity

Why on earth do you want to lug around all that excess baggage? It doesn't make sense, but you say, "I can't help myself." "My metabolism is different." "I have a glandular disease." "My family has always had this problem." On and on and on. Nonsense! I don't want to offend you, but there are few good excuses for obesity. Look at reality. You just eat too much. You are killing yourself. If that is what you want to do, there

everything they do. Many develop bad habits, which are pushed to the limit. If they smoke, they light up one after another, dragging compulsively on each cigarette and leaving no butt. They inhale and exhale impatiently and repetitively until a cloud that would set off a smoke alarm surrounds them. With all this intensity, what happens to blood pressure? Right! It rises. And it probably stays up. No time for a healthful, relaxed meal? Send out for one of those quick gourmet hamburgers and fries, capped off with a malt. Only 1,200 calories with 40 percent fat, so it slides down quick and easy. Hell, no time to think about the fact that Dad died of a heart attack at fifty-five. "It can't happen to me. I've got too much to do. I don't have time for a heart attack."

Second, there is growing evidence that the Type A personality, in and of itself, isn't necessarily bad. What kind of Type A you are may be the critical factor. A Type A who is truly happy and optimistic, who knows how to love himself and others, appears to be far less likely to develop heart disease, even if he is ambitious, time-oriented, and compulsive about things that are not self-destructive. Type A's who have difficulty manifesting or feeling love, who are short on compassion, who are rigid and uncompromising, who are self-centered and quick to anger, may be the Type A's who are most likely to suffer from heart disease.

The Iowa businessman who dissected his aorta was searching in vain for happiness. Somehow, what he had wasn't enough. So he drove himself, seeking more money, more success. He smoked too much. He ate too much. Still, he wasn't at peace. I think that's one of the big problems in our society today. People are not at peace with themselves. They're not healthy

205

spiritually. They're not healthy emotionally. And they become unhealthy physically.

Today, women are falling into the trap, too, driving too hard to achieve success in their careers. We're operating on women in their sixties and seventies now, but it's only a matter of time before we start seeing younger women in their forties and fifties. We're already seeing more ulcers and lung cancer among women. It makes no difference whether you're a man or a woman: Bad habits, plus bad attitudes, plus Type A personality equals narrow pipes to the heart.

Age

As one grows older, he or she is more at risk of having blocked blood vessels. It's a fact of life. Resign yourself. Go off, sit in a nursing home, and wait for the big one. Wait. And wait. Wait to die. That seems to be what happens to far too many. If you haven't traveled down that hopeless road yet, if you're still active— young or old—then listen: Try not to become a nursing home vegetable. Prevent it. Fight it as much as possible. Stay active, optimistic, helpful to others. Stay productive and maintain your physical body strength through diet and exercise. Then, as you develop heart ailments and other dreaded diseases, you'll be able to fight them. You'll be able to go through extensive surgery and recover to carry on your life again. Yes, age is a risk factor, but you don't have to let it consume you with hopelessness. I say this because it is true. I have seen it. Here is a marvelous example:

The gourmet meal looked scrumptious as I was about to sit down with my colleagues at a medical seminar. I was looking forward to the evening—good food and good white wine (in moderation, of course), a chance to hear a respected speaker describe advances in medical technology, and a chance to visit with my colleagues in a relaxed, informal atmosphere.

My beeper went off. Bad news. It was the cath lab. They wanted me, now! I got up reluctantly, leaving that marvelous meal untouched, and strode to a telephone, almost wishing I had chosen a different occupation. It would be nice to duck one of these calls just once, I thought. But of course, I couldn't. I dialed the lab. The phone rang once. The voice on the other end was short and authoritative: "Dr. Grooters, we need you right away. Dr. Charlotte Fisk is on the table, dying of a rupturing aorta right above the heart."

God! I thought with selfish disbelief. *She's eighty-four. Why are they even considering surgery?* I knew the woman, a tiny, retired pediatrician with a curvature of the spine that would make a pretzel look straight. To my way of thinking, it was probably time for her to die gracefully without heroic efforts to extend her life.

As I arrived at the cath lab, her blood pressure was low, in the 60s systolic, but she was still alert. Amazingly, she was still a fireball! I didn't realize this, however, until I told her what I thought was wrong: A huge aneurysm of the ascending aorta had dissected, in my opinion, and was bleeding into the sac around her heart. The pressure from the blood was compressing her heart and causing her shocklike condition. She couldn't last long.

The cardiologist was in the process of placing a needle into the sac to drain off some of the blood. As he did, I asked Dr. Fisk if she wanted me to try to fix her condition. Since she was eighty-four years old, I fully expected her to decline the operation. I thought she would decide that her time had come: a massive loss of blood, a quiet, painless, dignified end to a long, productive life.

Boy, was I wrong! Her answer was explosive and to the point: "Hell, yes! I don't have an alternative, other than dying, do I?"

"True," I acknowledged, more than a bit chastised and taken aback.

"Then get me to O.R. and fix me. I still have a lot of living to do."

There was no doubt. I was going to work tonight. And I did. Boy, did I work. The surgery required replacing not only the ascending aorta but all of the related vessels going to the brain. We had to use deep hypothermia and circulatory arrest for thirty minutes to preserve her brain while the new graft and brain vessels were attached.

I doubted she would wake up when we were done. She surprised me again. By the next morning, she was not only awake, she was raring to go. As soon as the endotracheal tube was removed from her throat, she pointedly asked about the University of Iowa's basketball team: "Did the Hawkeyes win?"

What a remarkable person living in that twisted, tiny body! I call her the strongest person in town. Today, she is back doing volunteer work. She drives her car to meetings around town, even though she has to peer through the slit between the top of the steering wheel and the dashboard to see where she's going. I see her every Sunday in church and almost feel guilty every time for not having higher expectations about her ability to survive and thrive. She is a survivor, and a thriver, and an inspiration to us all.

Yes, you can be knocked down when you get older, and you can get back up and go again.

Gender

It has been well known for some time that men have more coronary problems than women. The ratio may be about ten to one. But once women reach menopause, they rapidly develop more risk. By the time women reach sixty five, the men-to-women risk ratio may be diminished to about three to one.

Ten years ago, I operated on ten men for every one woman. Today, my ratio is more like four to one. There may be many reasons for this: more women working in high-stress jobs, more women smoking than before. Whatever the reasons, the point is, heart disease risks are rising for women relative to men. So women, don't ignore your heart! You are not immune from this affliction, particularly as you get older.

There's another more subtle sex-related difference between men and women. Women have a higher mortality rate and receive less long-term benefit from surgery. Yes, men get the disease more often than women, but women have a tougher time with it when they get the disease. The average risk of dying in heart surgery is about 1 percent for men, but 2 percent or more for women.

It's not clear why women are at greater risk in surgery, but it may have something to do with the fact that their coronary arteries are much smaller, more active, and technically more demanding to operate on. Their arteries can spasm or squeeze down to smaller sizes more quickly, which may lead to failure of the bypasses a surgeon puts in.

Previous Heart Attack and/or Surgery

If you've had a heart attack, an angioplasty, or open-heart surgery, you need to be very aware of your health. Schedule frequent checkups, at least yearly. Know your body and how it should feel. Don't ignore warning signs. There's a tendency among heart surgery patients to think, "Now I'm fixed, I made it." Be careful! You are not cured. You are only bypassed. Nothing more. Or you have only survived a heart attack. Nothing more. One of the biggest mistakes we see occurs among people who are two, maybe three years away from their open-heart surgery and forget all about it. They revert to their old habits. They ignore their blood pressure. Their waistlines balloon again. They start smoking again. And then they can't believe it when they're having a heart attack! After all, we fixed them, right? The truth is, surgeons don't cure the disease. They only bypass it and give the patient more time. How much more time? It varies with each individual, but generally speaking the death rate after the operation is 1 percent per year for the first five years and about 2 percent per year between five and ten years after surgery. If you have a damaged heart muscle from a previous heart attack, your risk of dying may be three times as high. If you have disease throughout your vessels, your risk is at least three times as high. If you revert back to your old habits, your risk rises again. How much? Who knows!

So modify your behavior. Take care of yourself, and

not just in the first two or three years after heart surgery but for the rest of your life. If you have a recurrence of symptoms, *do not ignore them. You may be in extreme danger!* Come back before it's too late. If we have to open you up a second time, the risk is quadrupled. But that's still better than dying before help arrives. And it's still better than emergency surgery, where your chance of dying can be as high as one in five.

The Heart I Can't Fix

The call came from the cardiologist about midafternoon: "We've got a man here, mid-fifties. You'd better take a look at his angiogram."

"You'd better." Those words raised the red flag in my mind. I went right to the cardiac catheterization lab, where I found an ugly picture of a severely diseased heart with blockages in all of the arteries to the heart. The picture put this man around the 20 to 25 percent fatal heart attack per year risk level. Perhaps even higher, because he'd been hospitalized with chest pain, shortness of breath, and fatigue. He was a definite candidate for surgery. Despite all his problems, I thought we could really help him. In fact, it really looked quite easy. His arteries were big, making the bypass operation easy and increasing our chances for success.

I entered the man's room, feeling optimistic about this "easy" case, to find a man sitting bolt upright in bed, intense and demanding, as if he might jump up at any moment. He was trying to present a commanding attitude. Yet, when I shook his hand, his palm was sweaty, his grip was shaky and weak. Outwardly, he seemed in control, but it was obvious that he was worried and insecure. His smile was tense and artificial. His voice was tight.

I'd barely introduced myself and was about halfway into the chair by his bed when he started: "Doc, all I want you to do is fix my heart and get me out of here. My business is going good. I'm about to make a lot of money. Just give me four or five years to enjoy it. Don't tell me about the surgery. I don't want to know. Just fix me and get me out of here."

There was tremendous tension and anxiety in his voice as he went on to explain the things he had to do before he died—run his speedboat, finish building his house, see his grandchildren for a few more years, get his business to the point where he'd have all the money he would ever need

I let him ventilate for maybe five minutes, appearing to listen intently, although the details he related weren't important. I'd already observed what I needed to know. His performance was pathetic. It was maddening to see this grown man with a sick heart so crippled by short-term thinking, so obsessed with immediate goals. It struck me, as he proceeded with his list of demands from life, that he needed more than the cut of my knife.

Just a few weeks earlier, during a special weekly course at church, I'd run across a Taoist verse that rang so true, I immediately committed it to memory. I tore a blank piece of paper out of his chart, the page where we normally write progress notes. And while the man continued his ventilations, I jotted down this verse:

> Those who flow as life flows know
> they need no other force.
> They feel no wear, they feel no tear.
> They need no mending, no repair.

I looked him straight in the eye and said, "I know you need heart surgery, but let me share something with you," and I handed him that verse. As I handed it to him, I said, "You know, you need to slow down a little bit. I think you need to learn how to be content." I tried to be kind but firm.

It took him by surprise. He read the verse and then put the paper down and agreed to converse about the surgery, to listen while I explained to him the benefits and risks of surgery. Before I left the room, I said, "Read that verse over some more and think about it." As I walked to the door, I thought his chances of taking the verse to heart were maybe one in ten.

Later that afternoon, as I was walking past his room to see another patient, he stopped me and said, "I need to tell you something. I called my wife and read her that verse. She laughed and said, 'You need that more than anyone I know, but there is no way you can live by that verse.'

"I think my wife is wrong," he said. "I've been thinking about it, and I am going to live that way if you can get me through surgery."

His surgery was successful. He was healthy and able to leave the hospital five days after the bypass surgery. He had a great deal of enthusiasm. He seemed uplifted. It almost seemed as if his spirit was flying like an eagle.

I've seen him several times in the years since his surgery. He looks good and healthy. He looks much happier and relaxed, almost as if he's found heaven on earth. And each time I see him, he says to me, "I'm still with the flow."

With the flow. How many of us are with the flow? It seems not many in this day and age. We live the way we drive. Have you ever noticed how we drive? Have you observed us on the streets, freeways, and highways? We speed. We run red lights. We crowd the center

214

line. We tailgate. We honk when we have to wait a moment. We swerve in and out of traffic. We drive aggressively, using our cars almost like weapons to save two minutes or less.

We work the same way—always trying to get ahead, to do a bit more than those around us, to get "one up." I see it in my own profession—doctors who spend all their time at the hospital. You don't know if it's because they don't want to be home around their families, if they're obsessed with work, or if they just don't know how to relax and enjoy life, to go with the flow. Whatever the reasons, they wind up in a high-stress trap that ends up running their lives and hurting their hearts. I know. Until a few years ago, I was one of those doctors. I lived and worked that way. I'm human, too, and God knows I was like that. I have to watch it still, or I'll be that way again. Every now and then, I have to repeat that poem and laugh at myself, and think, *Oh vanity of vanities!*

Go with the flow, as you read this "Desiderata" by Max Ehrmann. I read it for the first time on a Christmas card from dear friends of our family. I've saved the card for the last twenty years, and I still read it whenever my life starts pushing against the stream. I hope it helps you as much as it has helped me:

Desiderata*

Go placidly amid the noise and the haste, and remember what peace there may be in silence. As far as possible without surrender be on good terms with all persons.

Speak your truth quietly and clearly; and listen to others, even the dull and ignorant; they too have their story.

Avoid loud and aggressive persons, they are vexations to the spirit.

If you compare yourself with others you may become vain and bitter; for always there will be greater and lesser persons than yourself.

Enjoy your achievements as well as your plans. Keep interested in your own career, however humble; it is a real possession in the changing fortunes of time.

Exercise caution in your business affairs; for the world is full of trickery. But let this not blind you to what virtue there is; many persons strive for high ideals; and everywhere life is full of heroism.

Be yourself. Especially do not feign affection. Neither be cynical about love; for in the face of all aridity and disenchantment it is as perennial as the grass.

Take kindly the counsel of the years, gracefully surrendering the things of youth. Nurture strength of spirit to shield you in sudden misfortune. But do not distress yourself with imaginings. Many fears are born of fatigue and loneliness. Beyond a wholesome discipline, be gentle with yourself. You are a child of the universe no less than the trees and the stars; you have a right to be here. And whether or not it is clear to you,

no doubt the universe is unfolding as it should. There-
fore be at peace with God, whatever you conceive Him
to be. And whatever your labors and aspirations, in the
noisy confusion of life keep peace with your soul.

With all its sham, drudgery and broken dreams, it
is still a beautiful world. Be cheerful. Strive to be happy.

—Max Ehrmann

That does not mean that we can't work hard, that
we can't accomplish things in a competent, compassionate, forgiving manner. Some people live that way
naturally. My mother has that natural grace. She lets
life flow. Her father, my grandpa, had natural grace,
too. A self-educated immigrant from Holland who
learned English by reading the Bible, he had the stocky
build of a bulldog and the grace of a saint. He was a
very pragmatic, temperate man. He didn't believe in
abstinence. He believed in temperance. Everything
could be enjoyed in moderation. That may not be quite
right, but that's what he believed, and he got a kick out
of preaching that philosophy among our strict,
abstinence-minded Dutch Reformed family and
friends. His favorite example was Christ turning water
into wine. If wine was so wrong, then why would God
make more?

He was a very patient man with a tremendous
sense of humor. He could laugh at almost anything. I
remember, one time when I was five or six years old, I
ran up behind Pete Van Zee, one of Grandpa's friends,
and bonked him on the head with my little toy hammer.
I took off running and an enraged Van Zee took off after
me. Around and around we went near my grandpa's
blacksmith shop while Grandpa stood and laughed
with tears running from his eyes. He enjoyed the sight
of this little kid being chased by a big, enraged, burly

man. He wasn't angry. Yet, when it was all over and my grandfather had his hands on me, it didn't take me long to realize that I'd done wrong. The pinch on my arm told me I'd done wrong. I knew, when my grandpa took that hammer, that I would never see it again. And I didn't.

I was always very proud of that man. Unlike my father, who wanted me to go to college, Grandpa would let me work in the family blacksmith shop, would patiently teach me how to do things and let me make mistakes. I still remember how he taught me to weld by handing me two pieces of metal. "Go ahead," he said. "See how you can do." I worked slowly and carefully, welding the two pieces with fine, neat seams. It looked pretty good. Grandpa took it, tapped it on the anvil, and it fell apart. What better way for me to learn that I hadn't taken the time to heat the two pieces, to meld them together. Grandpa was patient enough to let me make the mistake, to teach me the importance of doing things right. I didn't realize it at the time, but that patience, that grace, is what I had always admired.

My grandpa's welding lesson applies to life as well; we have to live our lives right, or they'll fall apart. For my grandpa, the balance, grace, and inner peace seemed to come naturally. Most of the rest of us have to work at it. We need to realize that if the inner heart is sick, it can make the physical heart sick as well. The heart is the primary target of stress. It has to pump against the tension. Medical science can't measure the daily damage, but it accumulates relentlessly, week after week, year after year, decade after decade, until the heart breaks down.

Don't try to force life through. Go with the flow. This society is so impatient. It needs more of that philosophy. We need to be content. But how can we be content, going 100 miles per hour all the time, looking for pleasure. It's no wonder we have so many health problems. Our approach to life is not healthy.

We all have our limits, especially in a physical sense. The heart I work on, the physical heart, is no exception. What I have seen during more than 4,000 heart surgeries is the late stages of the physical disease, the prefatal stage of heart disease. In many cases, thanks to the wonders of modern medicine, I can fix the physical heart with bypass surgery. I cannot fix the other heart, the inner heart. No surgeon can. And that heart, as much as we surgeons would like to believe otherwise, is the most important heart. Sure, you have to take care of yourself with a good diet, proper exercise, no smoking, moderate drinking. And the sooner you begin, the better. But most of the physical abuses—poor diet, lack of exercise, heavy smoking and drinking—are just symptoms of a sick inner heart, symptoms of a wrong attitude toward life, symptoms of going against life's flow.

Remember the Iowa businessman, the one who drove himself the way many of us drive our cars, the one who pushed his business and personal lives to the breaking point? Remember the elderly pediatrician, the twisted little woman who walked with dignity? The businessman was probably viewed with envy by many in his community—material wealth, prestige, and privilege. The pediatrician was viewed by many—including me, I'm sorry to say—as someone who had lived and suffered enough. Who, do you suppose, had the healthier inner heart at the moment I first encountered them for surgery? I'm sure you know. The pediatrician's inner heart needed no healing; the businessman's was in critical condition.

I once asked an eighty-three-year-old man after surgery, "How are you doing?"

"I'm doing fine," he replied, "but the house I live in is wearing out."

Doing fine. With the flow. Even near the end of his life on earth. A life shrouded with fear, greed, selfishness, and impatience makes earth hell. A heart, if used right; a life, if lived right, makes earth heaven.

Go with the flow.

Dr. Grooters's Informal Glossary
for Consumers

ACIDOTIC. Blood with too much acid in it, frequently caused by shock.

ADRENALIN, EPINEPHRINE. A potent substance used to stimulate the heart to do more work by beating faster and squeezing harder.

AIR EMOBOLIZATION. The introduction of air bubbles into the bloodstream, a dangerous condition because the bubbles can obstruct blood flow to the brain or other organs, sometimes causing strokes and significant damage.

AMICAR. A drug used to prevent a patient's own substances from dissolving blood clots.

ANGIOGRAM. An X ray of a blood vessel.

ANGIOPLASTY. Also called "percutaneous transluminal coronary angioplasty" (PCTA), or the "balloon procedure," where a balloon catheter is inserted in an artery to open the vessel by compressing built-up plaque.

AORTA. The main artery coming directly out of the heart, through the chest, and into the abdomen, where it divides to become two arteries going to the legs. It gives off many branches before it divides.

ARTERIAL BLOCKAGE. Obstruction of an artery, usually by fatty deposits called plaque.

ARTERIAL LINE FILTER. The filter in the tubing between the heart-lung machine and the patient to filter out microscopic particles.

ARTERIES. Vessels that carry oxygenated blood away from the heart to body tissues.

ATRIAL CLAMP. A special noncrushing clamp used on the

atrium of the heart to assist with the insertion of a cannula, or tube, into the atrium.

ATRIUM. One of two upper chambers of the heart.

BALLOON PROCEDURE. The insertion of a balloon catheter to open a narrowed blood vessel by compressing plaque buildups.

BASE DEFICIT. A condition in which the blood does not contain enough bicarbonate (pop fizz) to counteract acid.

BASE EXCESS. Too much bicarbonate in the blood.

BLOOD GASES. The measurement of oxygen and carbon dioxide levels in arterial blood.

BLOOD PRESSURE. The measured pressure inside a person's major blood vessels.

BLOOD REPLACEMENT PRODUCTS. Solutions and proteins other than blood used to replace a patient's blood volume. Also clotting factors.

BUBBLE OXYGENATOR. An apparatus attached to the heart-lung pump which oxygenates (puts oxygen into) the blood by bubbling oxygen through the blood.

BYPASS MACHINE. The heart-lung machine.

BYPASS SURGERY. Surgery used to bypass a defect or obstruction in a blood vessel. A good vessel taken from the leg or some other part of the body typically is spliced around the obstruction or problem in order to create a bypass, or detour, for blood flow.

CAT SCAN (Computer-Assisted Tomography). A computerized form of multiple X-ray pictures rapidly assembled to show internal body structures, usually used to diagnose problems in the brain, heart, or other organs and body parts.

C.P.R. (CardioPulmonary Resuscitation). The use of mouth-to-mouth resuscitation and manual pumping on the chest to produce blood pressure and keep the brain and other organs alive until medical help arrives.

CANNULA. A tube inserted into blood vessels.

CARDIAC CATHETERIZATION. A procedure in which a small tube

is inserted into the heart via blood vessels in the body. It is used to make measurements of pressures in the heart and to inject contrast material (dye) into coronary blood vessels to help find defects or obstructions.

CARDIAC SURGERY. Surgery of the heart.

CARDIOLOGIST. A doctor specializing in the diagnosis and nonsurgical treatment of heart ailments.

CARDIOPLEGIA. The cold (4 degrees centigrade) solution containing glucose and potassium used to cool the heart and preserve it.

CARDIOVASCULAR SYSTEM. The heart, lungs, and all of the blood vessels in the body.

CAROTID ENDARTERECTOMY. A surgical procedure used to remove plaque from the carotid artery.

CATH LAB. Abbreviation for the laboratory where a person's heart is studied.

CHOLESTEROL LEVEL. The amount of cholesterol in the blood. Levels above 200 could lead to a more frequent artery plaque buildup, blockage, and heart disease.

CONTRACTIBILITY. The amount of "squeeze," or work, the heart can do.

CORONARY ARTERIES. Arteries supplying the heart muscle.

CORONARY DISEASE. Blockages of the coronary arteries.

DIABETES. An illness that causes too much sugar in the blood from lack of insulin produced by the pancreas. Diabetes can make people more susceptible to heart disease because they have abnormal fat metabolism in the walls of their arteries.

DIASTOLIC. The lowest blood pressure recorded, when the heart is at rest between contractions.

DILATE. To stretch open.

DISSECTED AORTA. A condition in which the wall of the aorta is sheared into two thin layers by blood pushed between the layers. Often caused by high blood pressure, and often fatal.

DOBUTAMINE. Another epinephrine-like substance.

E.K.G. Electrocardiogram, an electric tracing of the heartbeat.

ELECTROSHOCK. Using an instrument to control electric current sent through the body to correct a rhythm disturbance of the heart or an emotional disturbance of the brain.

ENLARGED HEART. An abnormally large heart, usually indicating a significant heart ailment. The enlargement typically caused by the heart having to work too hard to keep blood pumping through the body. A very dangerous condition because of the stress it puts on the heart muscle.

ENDOTRACHEAL EQUIPMENT. Tools used to place a tube into a person's airway via the mouth.

FILMS. (1) "Movie-type" X rays of the heart or of the blood vessels; (2) plain X rays of a body part.

GENERAL SURGERY. A field that covers all types of surgeries, but mainly involving procedures within the abdomen such as appendectomies and hysterectomies.

GLUCOSE AND POTASSIUM SOLUTION. The cold, protective solution called "cardioplegia solution" used by heart surgeons to help protect and preserve the heart during surgery.

GRAFT. A new part stitched into an artery or other body part, either artificial or natural, from the same person, from another person, or from an animal.

HEART ATTACK. The loss of heart function and muscle, often caused by a coronary artery blockage cutting the supply of oxygen to the heart.

HEART DISEASE. The term used to connote serious ailments of the heart, often referring to blockages of coronary arteries due to the buildup of fatty plaque deposits.

HEART-LUNG MACHINE. A complex apparatus used to oxygenate blood and pump it through a patient during heart surgery and at other times when the heart can't handle the task.

HEMOGLOBIN. The oxygen-carrying protein in red blood cells.

224

HEPARIN A drug used to keep blood from clotting.

IV TUBE. A tube inserted into a vein to provide fluids with nourishment and/or medication to a person.

INFARCTION. The death of body tissue or an organ caused by an obstruction of local circulation.

INTERN. A young doctor in his or her first year of training after graduation from medical school.

INTERNAL MAMMARY ARTERIES. Two arteries in the chest located behind and on each side of the breastbone (sternum). It provides the best graft a surgeon can use to bypass arteries of the heart.

INTUBATION. To insert a tube into a body opening.

INTRA-AORTIC BALLOON PUMP. A timed pump with a special balloon inserted into the aorta to help a patient's heart pump.

MEMBRANE OXYGENATOR. The apparatus attached to the heart-lung machine which oxygenates (puts oxygen into) the blood while keeping the blood and gases separated with an artificial membrane.

MITRAL VALVE. The valve in the heart between the left atrium and the left ventricle.

NEONATAL. Newborn infants.

NITROGLYCERIN TABLETS. Small white pills placed under the tongue for chest pain (angina). The same compound used in explosives, it causes the arteries to dilate, or relax.

O.R. Operating room.

OFF PUMP. Slang indicating that a patient has been weaned from the heart-lung machine.

ON PUMP. Slang for a patient on a heart-lung machine whose heart and lungs are completely bypassed and not functioning.

OPERABLE. Someone who is "operable" is in good enough shape for surgery with a reasonable chance for success.

OSCILLOSCOPE. The monitor or screen on which information is displayed.

225

OXYGENATOR. An artificial apparatus used to put oxygen into the blood. An artificial lung.

PERFUSIONIST. The person who operates the heart-lung machine during heart surgery.

PERICARDIUM. The tough sac surrounding the heart.

PERIOPERATIVE INFARCATION. A heart attack or loss of heart muscle during or just after heart surgery.

PICTURE. An X ray, a film.

PLAQUE. The buildup of cholesterol and fat on the interior wall of an artery.

PROTAMINE. The drug used to reverse the anticoagulant, or blood-thinning, effect of heparin.

PULMONARY ARTERY. The vessel that brings unoxygenated blood from the right ventricle of the heart to both lungs.

PULSE "Ox." An instrument, usually attached to a fingertip or earlobe, used to provide continuous measurements of the amount of oxygen in the blood.

PULSE RATE. The number of beats, or pulses, per minute measured in a person. Somewhere between sixty and ninety beats per minute is usually considered normal.

RESIDENT. A doctor who has completed his or her internship and has entered advanced training for a specialty such as heart surgery.

RETRACTOR. An instrument used to retract or hold apart flesh or a wound so a surgeon can work.

SYSTOLIC. The peak blood pressure recorded when a person's heart is contracting.

STERNAL SAW. A saw used to cut the breastbone (sternum) in half, usually for heart surgery.

STERNUM. A person's breastbone, the hard bone in the front of the chest.

STROKE. Brain damage caused by a lack of blood circulation. Can be caused by a blockage or by a burst vessel.

SUTURES. Various types of threads with attached needles used to stitch tissue.

STAFF PHYSICIAN. A doctor with more experience than a resident who is a member of a hospital staff.

TRACHEOTOMY. A procedure to make an opening in the windpipe (trachea), often used to clear the windpipe and get air to a patient's lungs.

TYPE A PERSONALITY. An extremely competitive person, driven to excel, who strives hard to be perfect. There are whole books written on this one.

VASCULAR SURGERY. A specialty involving surgery on blood vessels, except for heart blood vessels.

VENA CAVA. The large veins that bring blood back to the heart, specifically the right atrium.

VENTRICLE. One of two lower chambers of the heart, which serve as the heart's main pumps.

WEANING PROCESS. The process of transferring a person's heart and lung functions from a bypass machine back to the person's own heart and lungs.